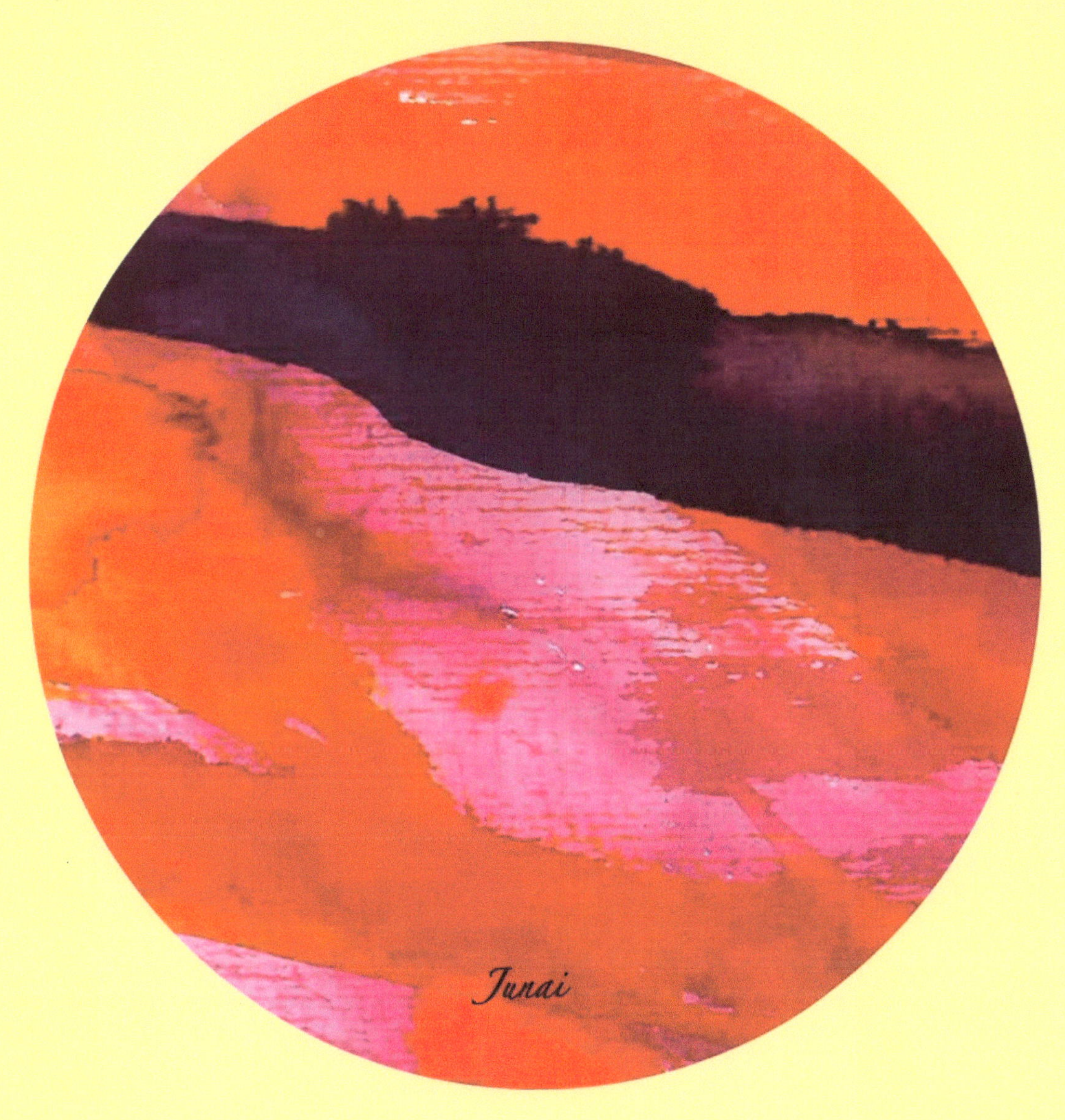

I am a Spirit

I am a Spirit, The ABCs of an Ideal Spirit

ISBN-13: 978-1-940736-25-9

For more information write:
QuickTurtle Books LLC
330 Schmid Rd
Fairview, Michigan 48621

Follow the Author Mary Rensberry at: maryrensberry.wordpress.com

Follow Artist Junai Meijer on Facebook at Junai Paintings & Art

Dedication

This book is dedicated to my mother.
I love you dearly, Mom.

Note from the Author

In many beliefs it is commonly held and agreed upon that we humans are tripartite, meaning, we are made up of body, mind and spirit. Its first known usage was around the 15th Century.

It is often stated that the spirit part of us is hard to understand and even comprehend. It is generally not written about nor talked about as being us. The mind has its own characteristics and proclivities as does the body. But it is the spirit that is Who We Are, the most essential part of who I am and who you are that reigns supreme. We are fully human, yet divine.

May you find this book filled with Truth and Beauty and may you rise to new heights on your continuing journey.

Acknowledgements

I'd like to acknowledge my husband, Richard, who is a source of inspiration to me. He always gives me his unparalleled advice especially in helping with this book. Above all, he's the best partner I could ask for.

Thanks to Junai Meijer, the illustrator, for her outstanding art and creativity. She and I were able to come together over the internet to put this book together out of a mutual passion to help others. Her watercolors are brilliant and captivating just as though you were walking through an enchanted garden.

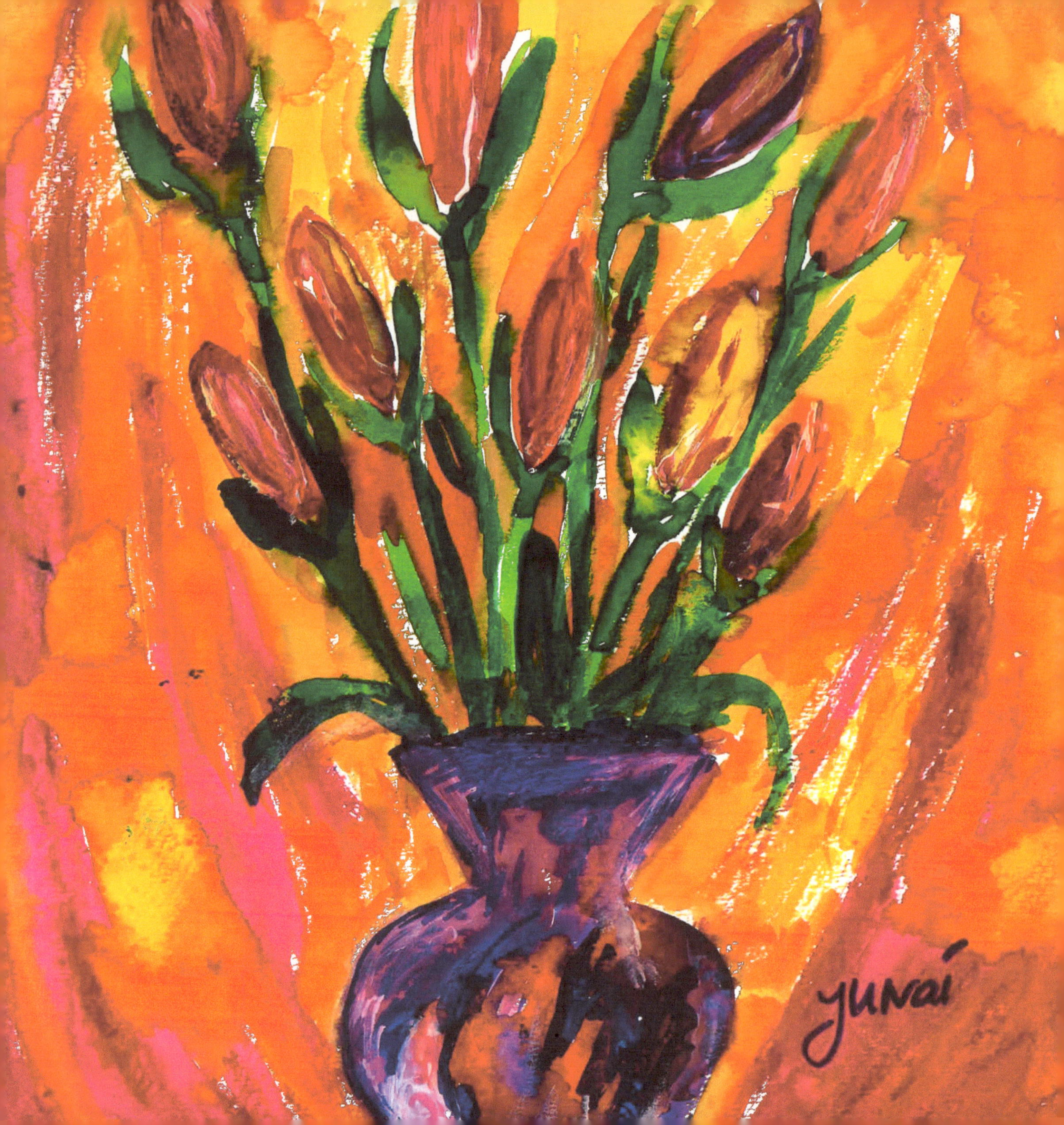
yunai

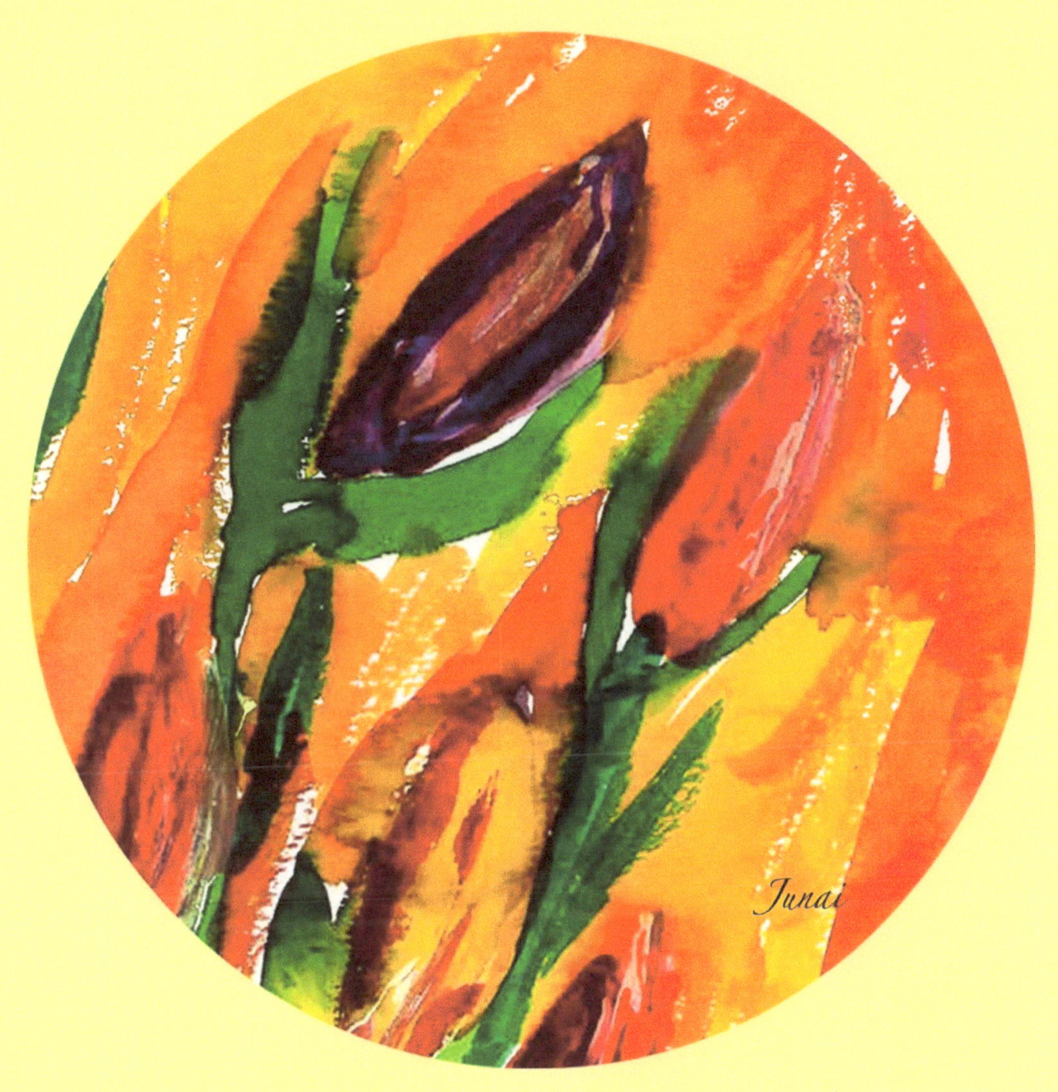

able

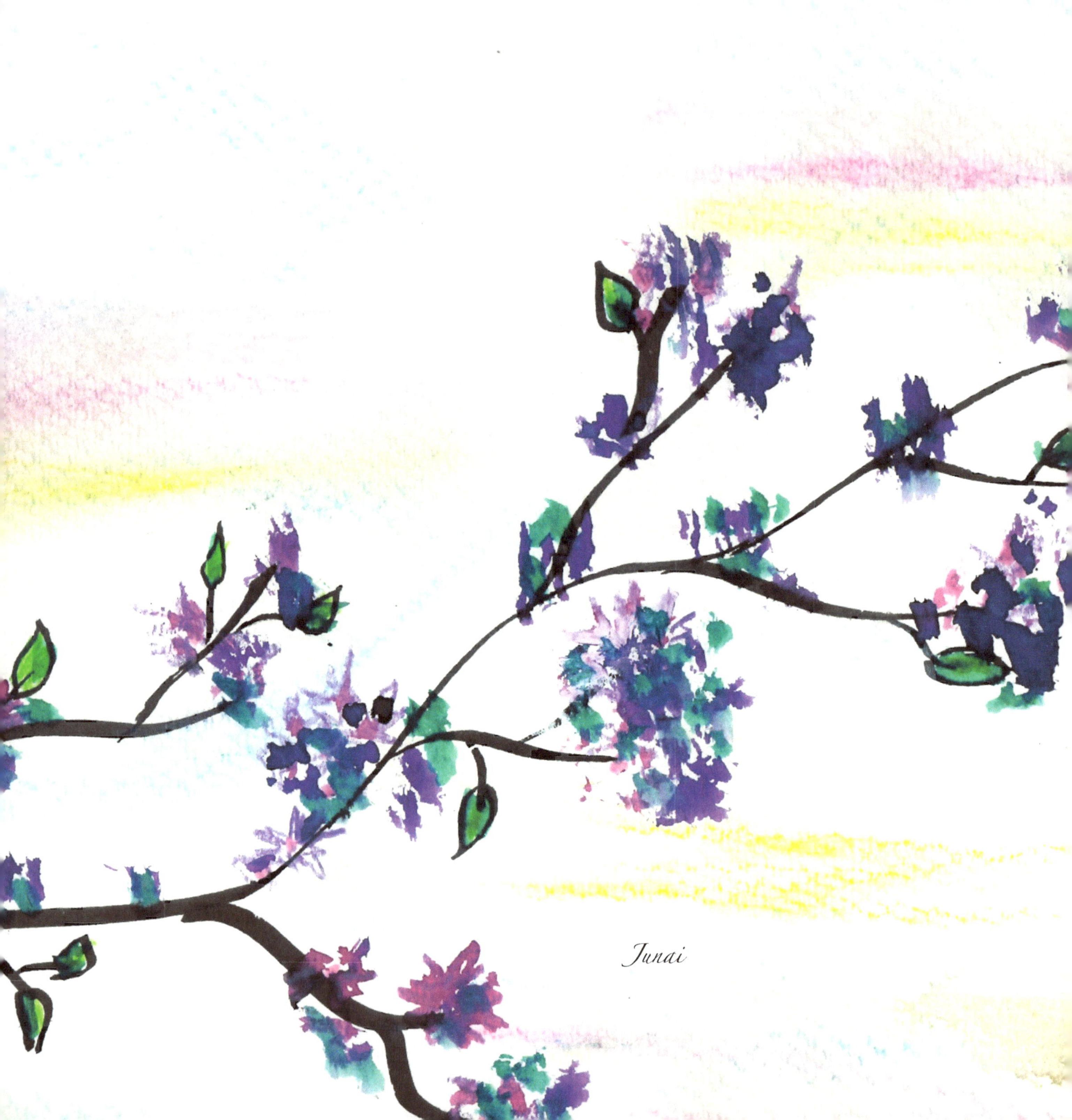
Junai

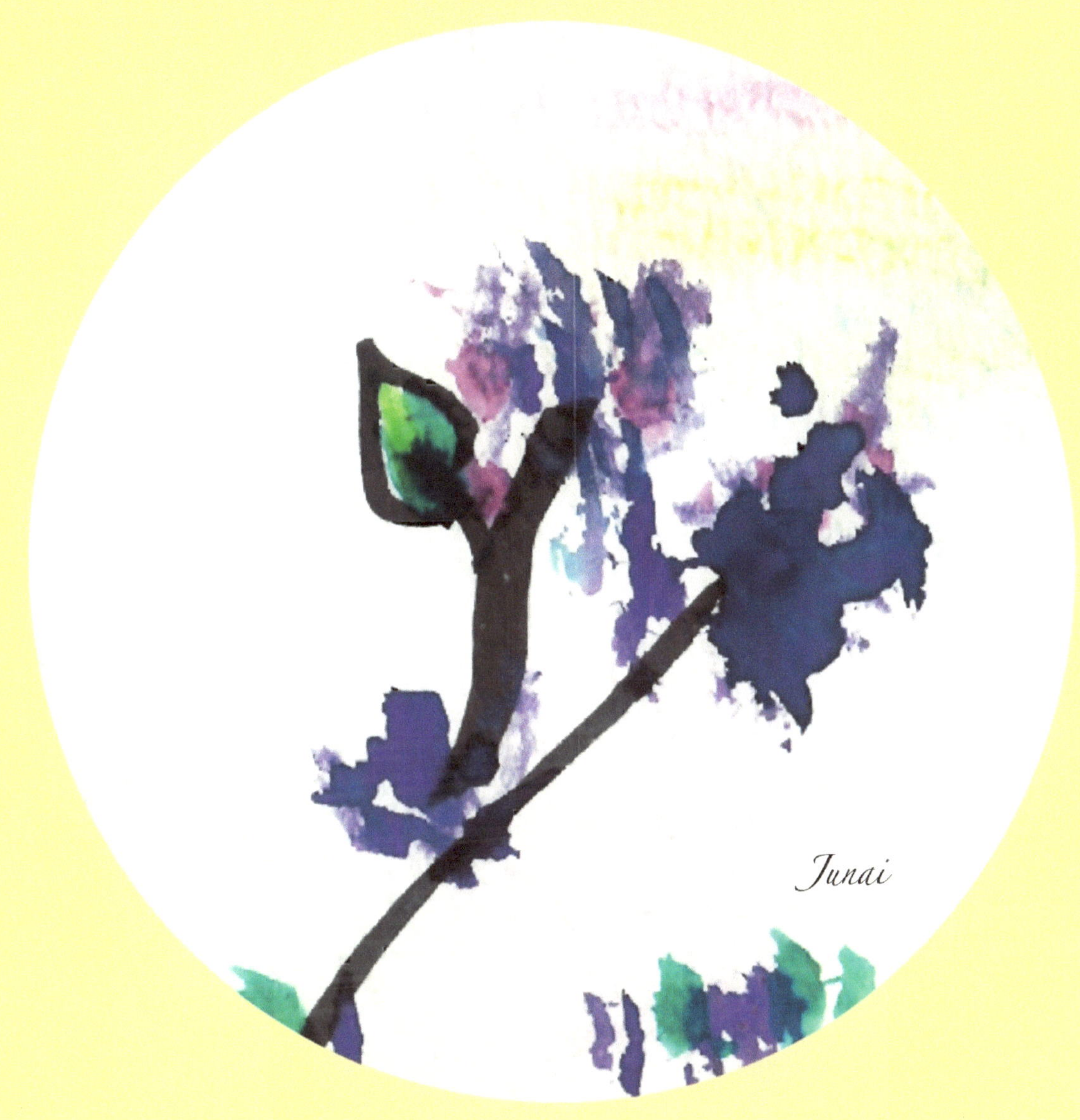

beautiful

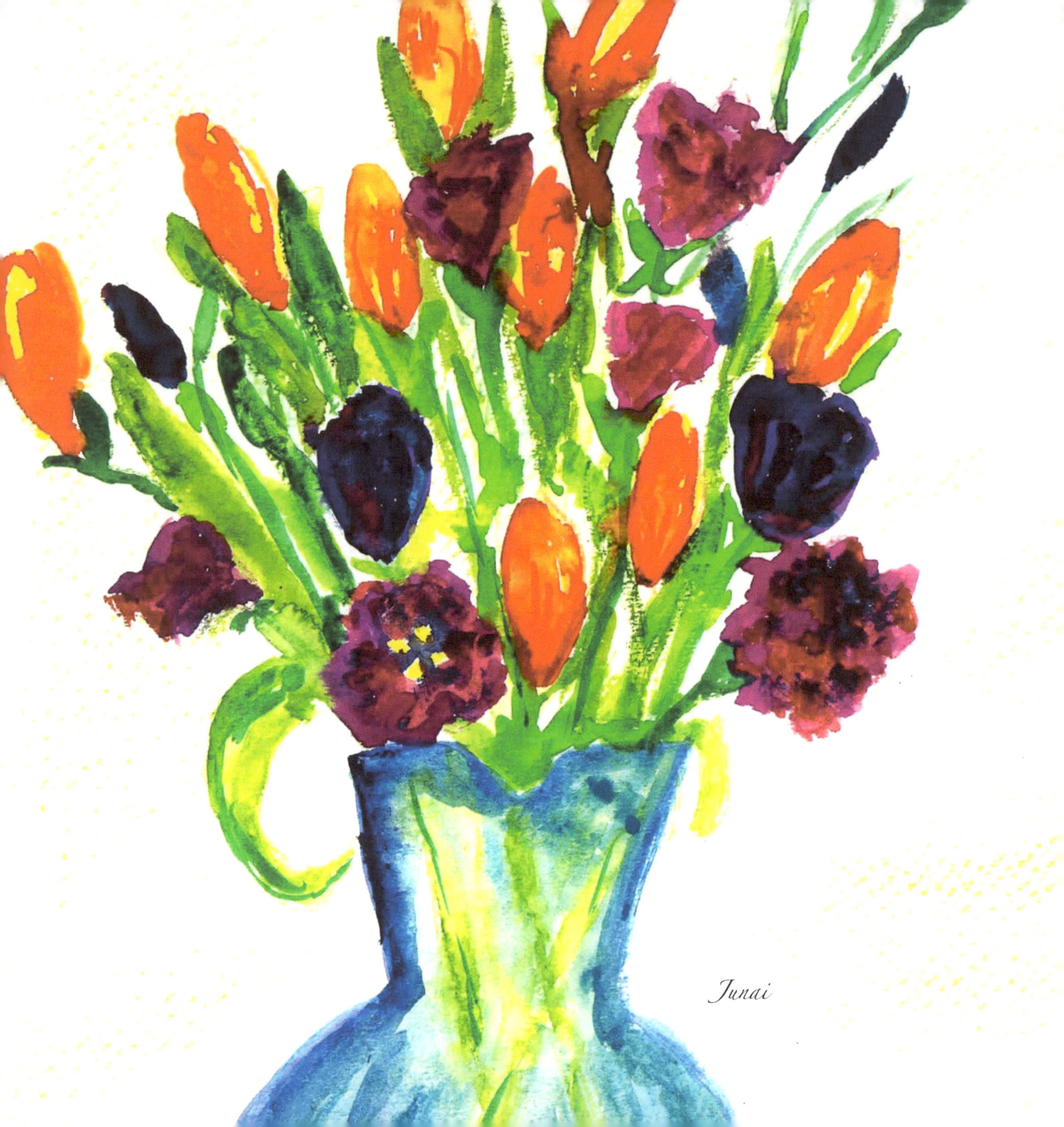
Junai

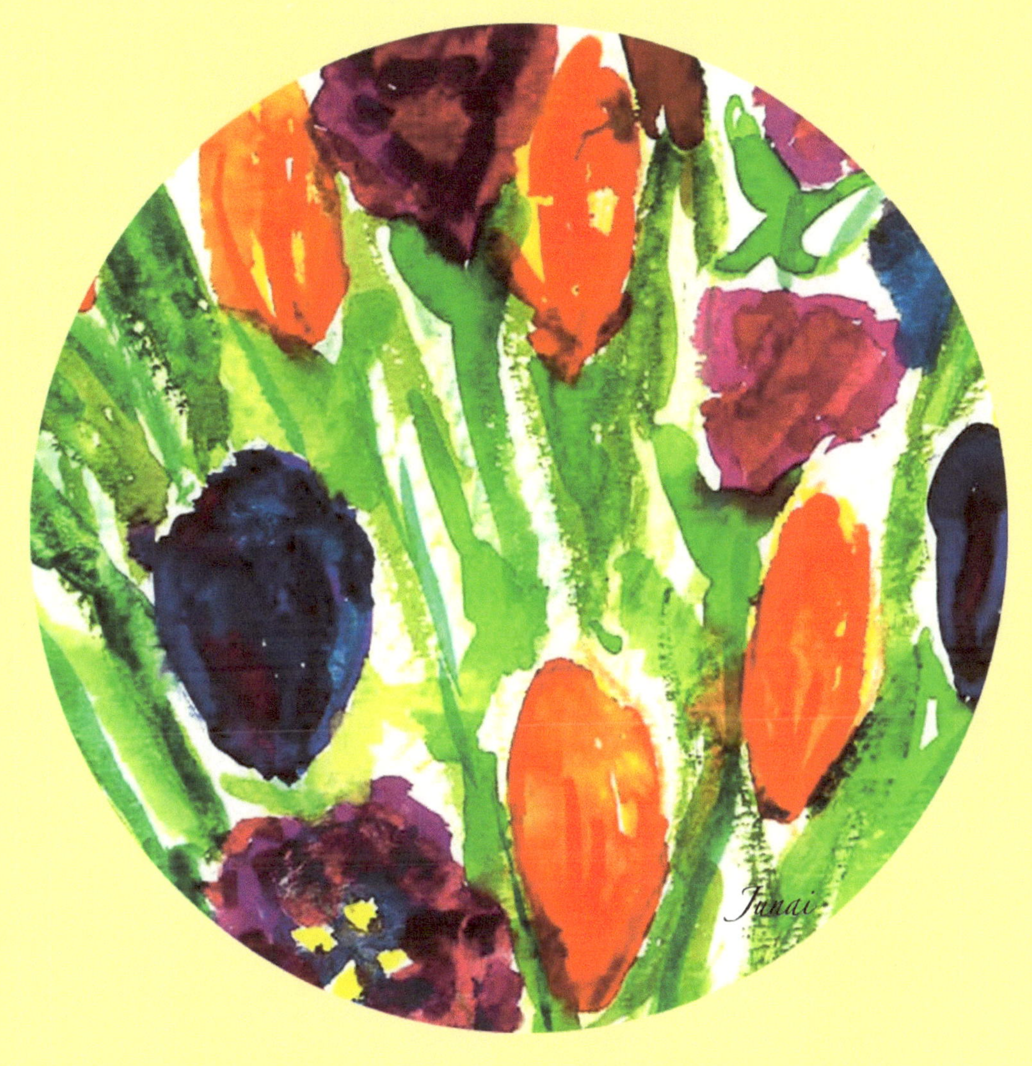

creative

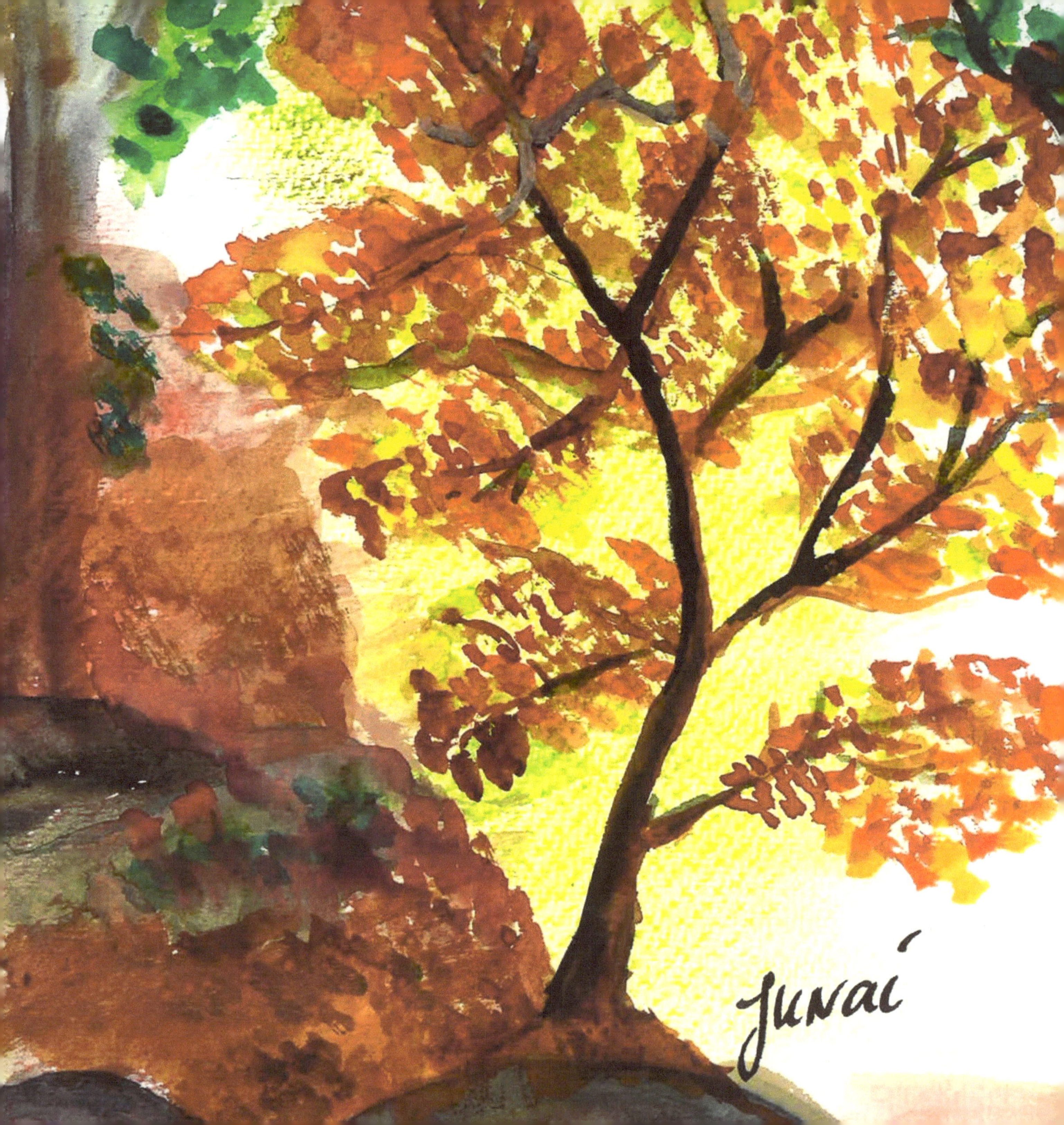
Junai

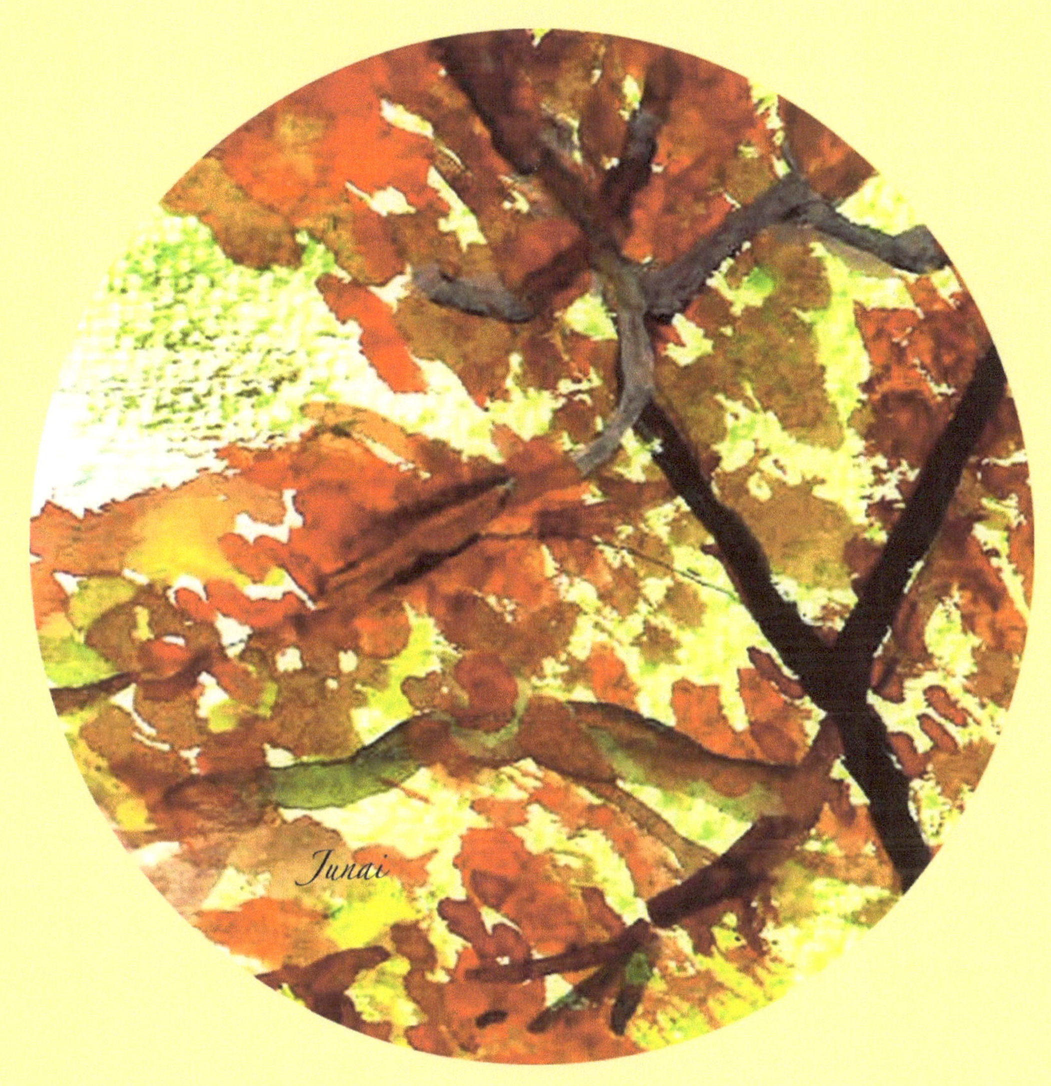

determined

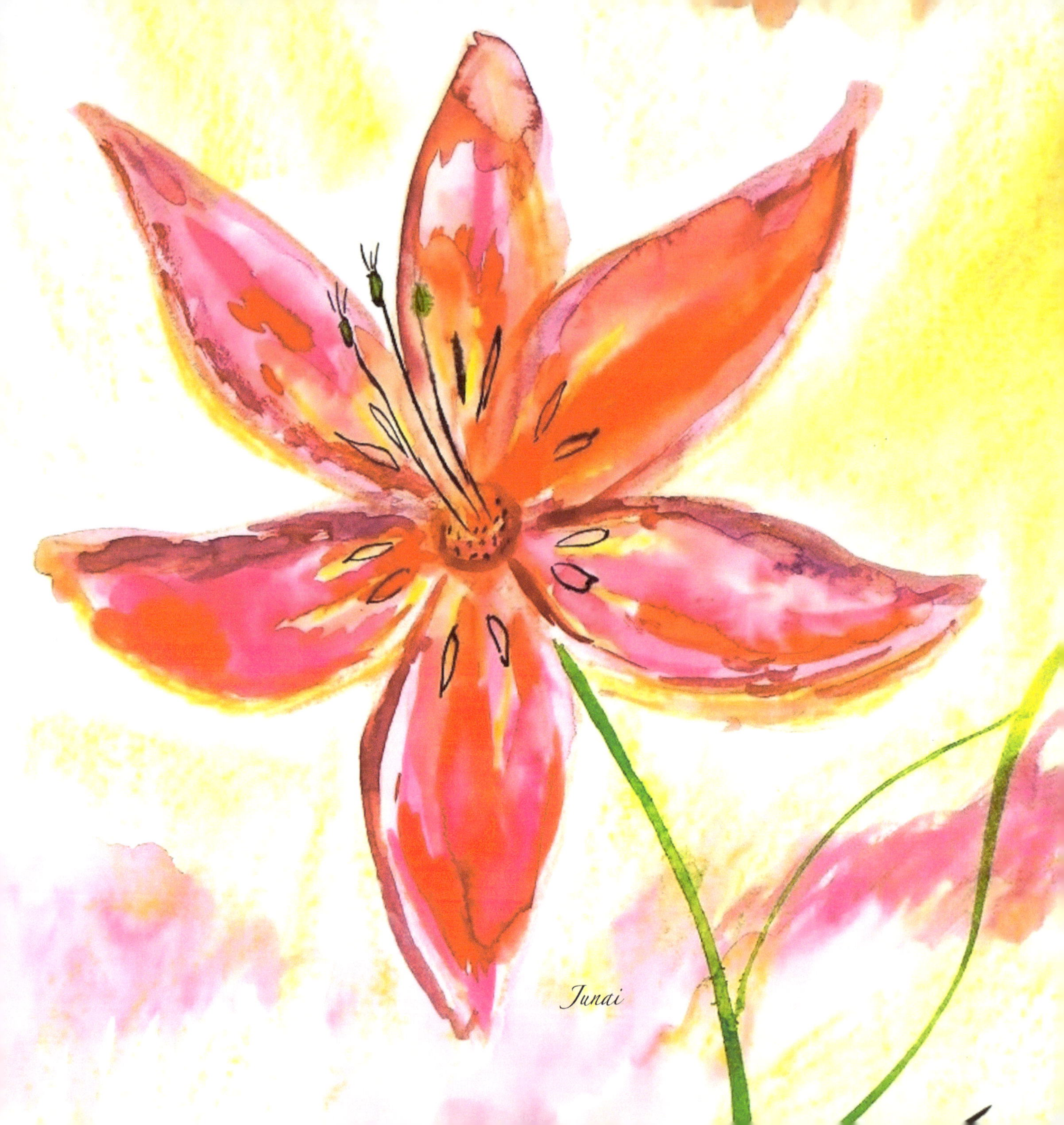
Junai

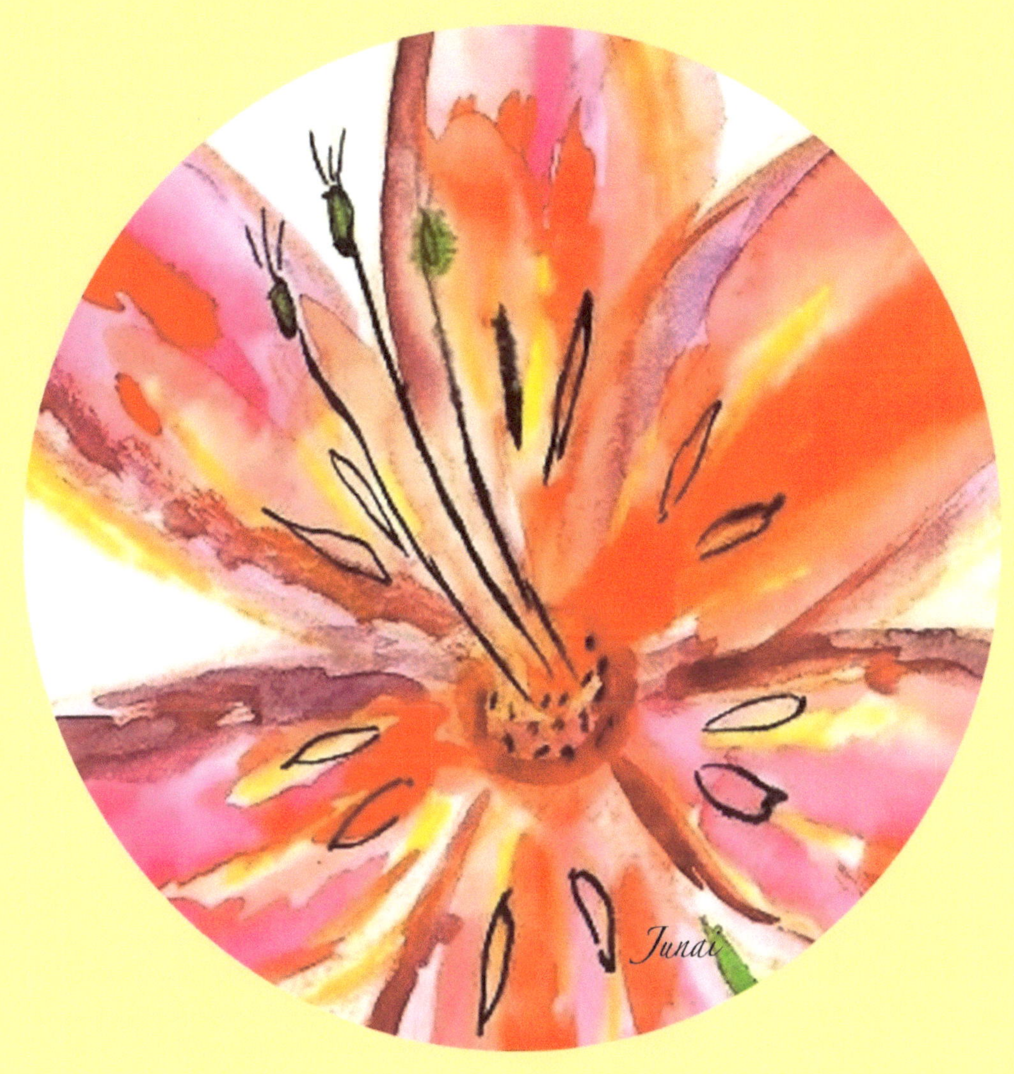

ethical

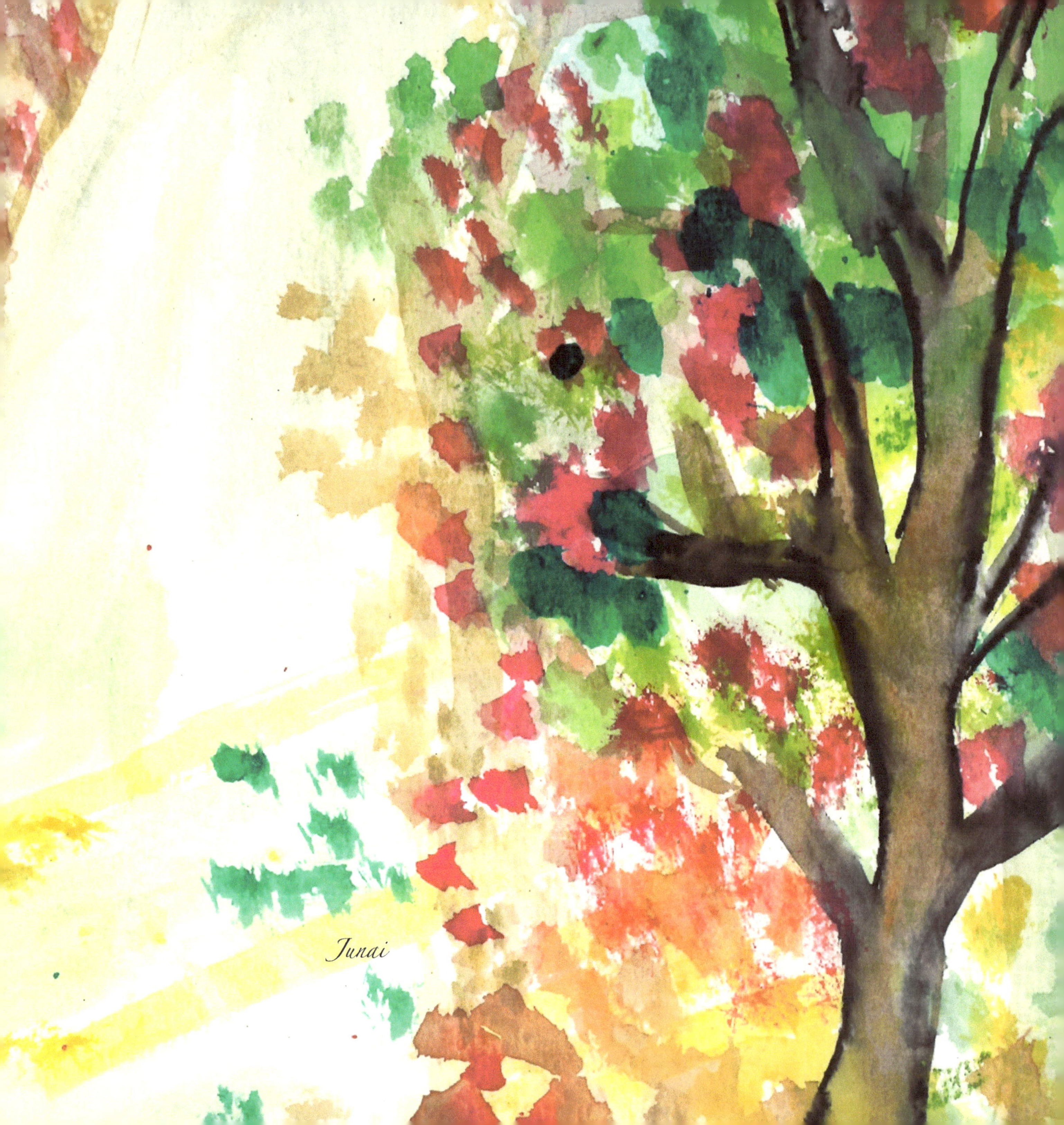
Junai

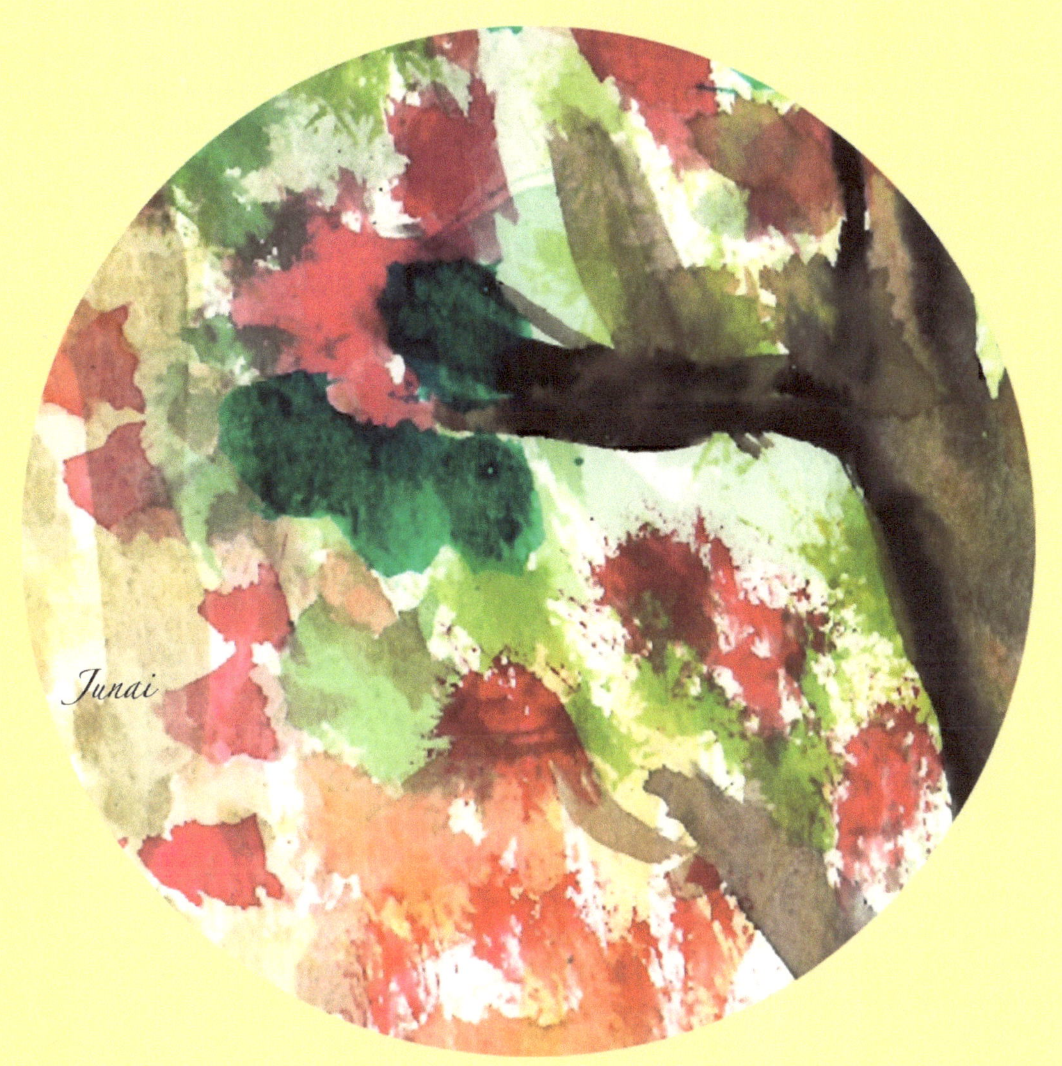

free

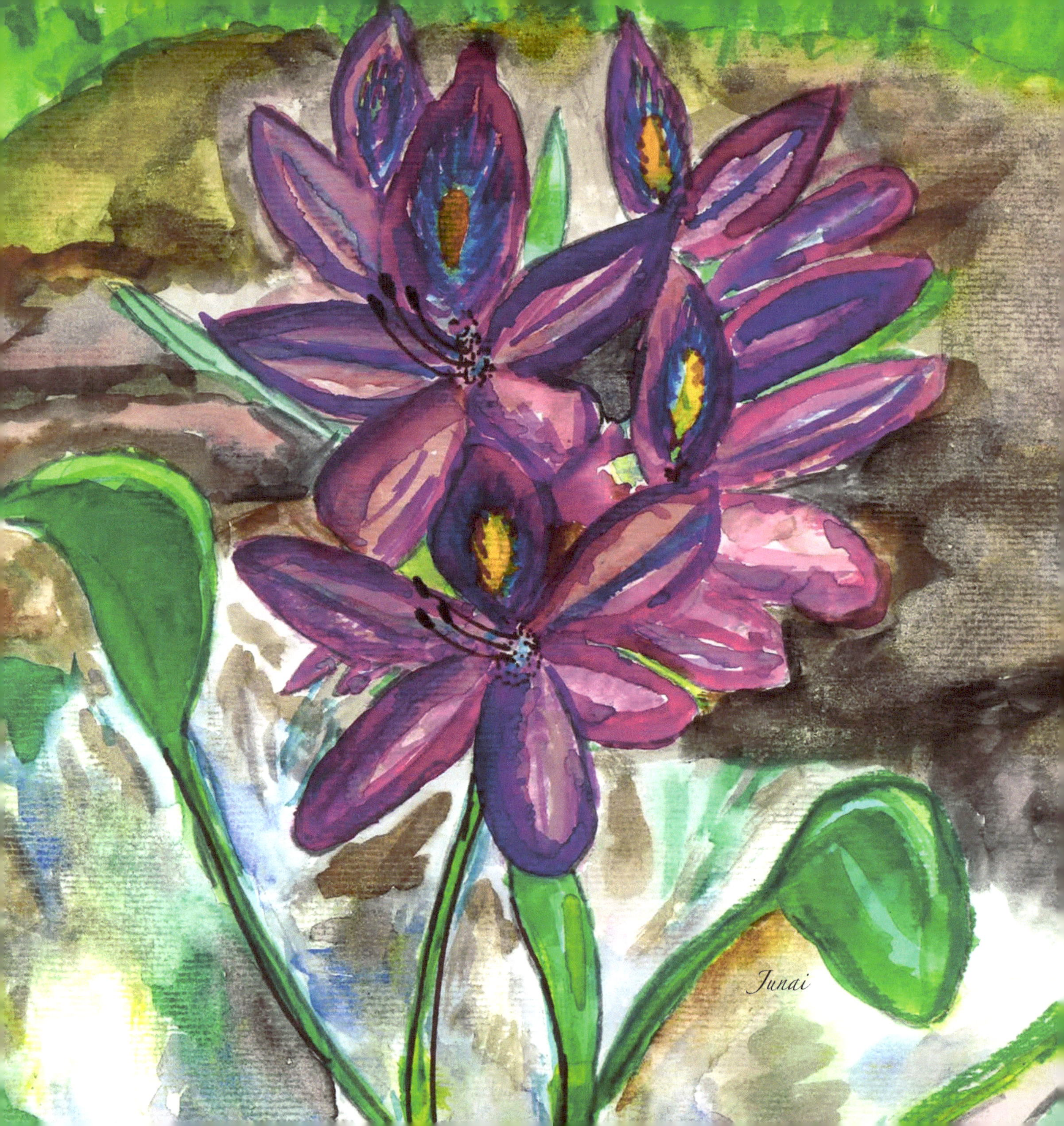
Junai

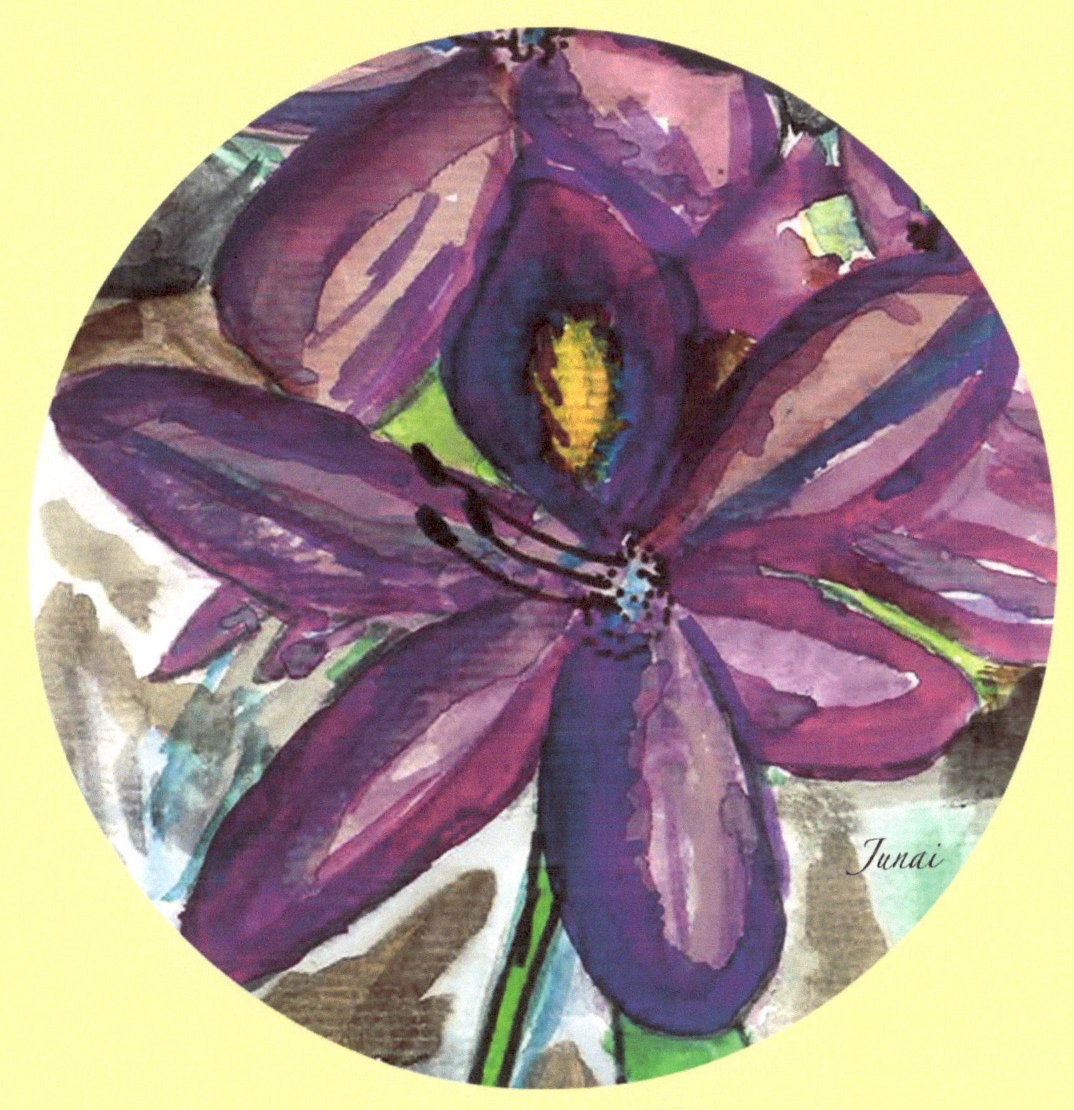

gracious

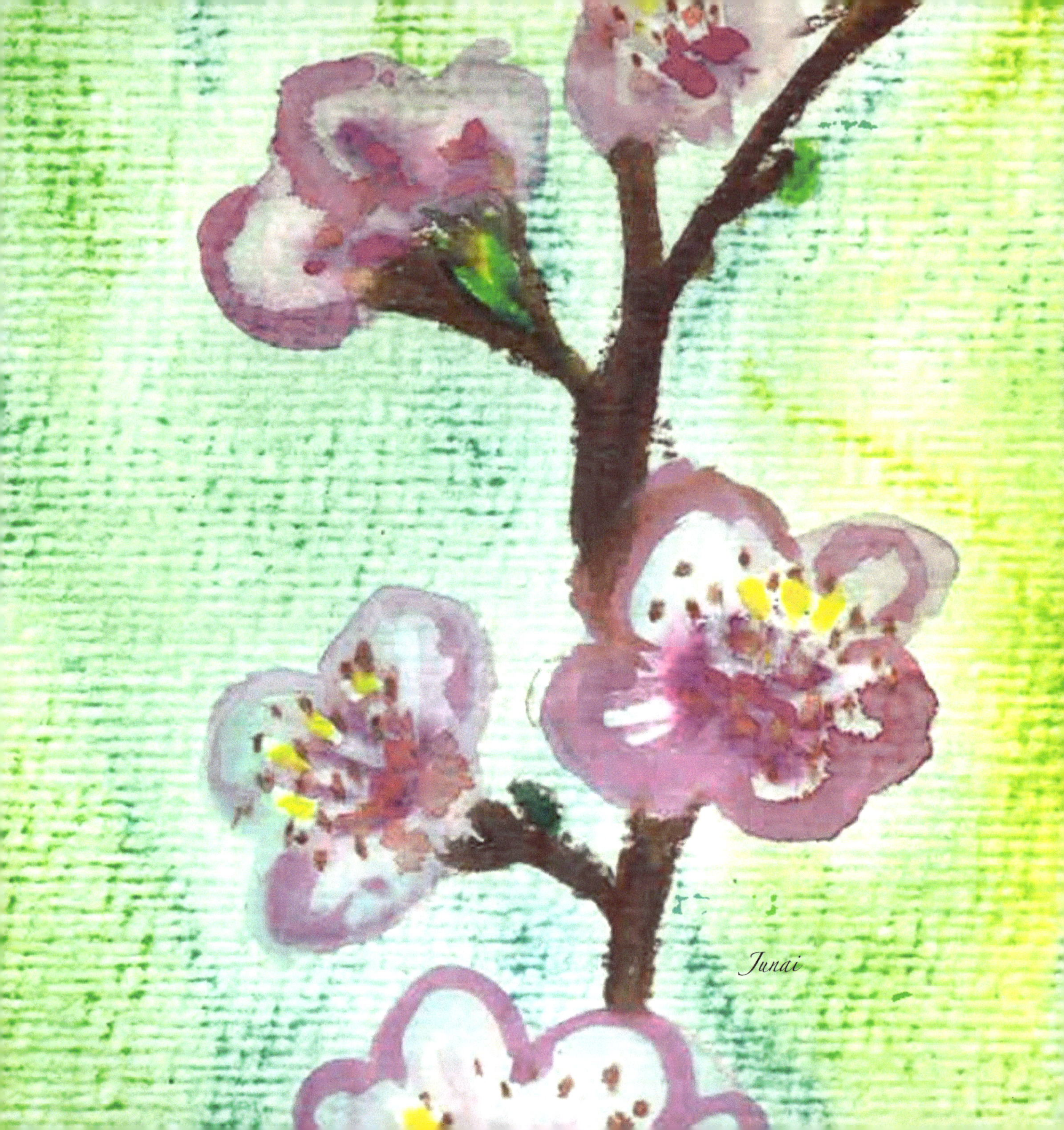
Junai

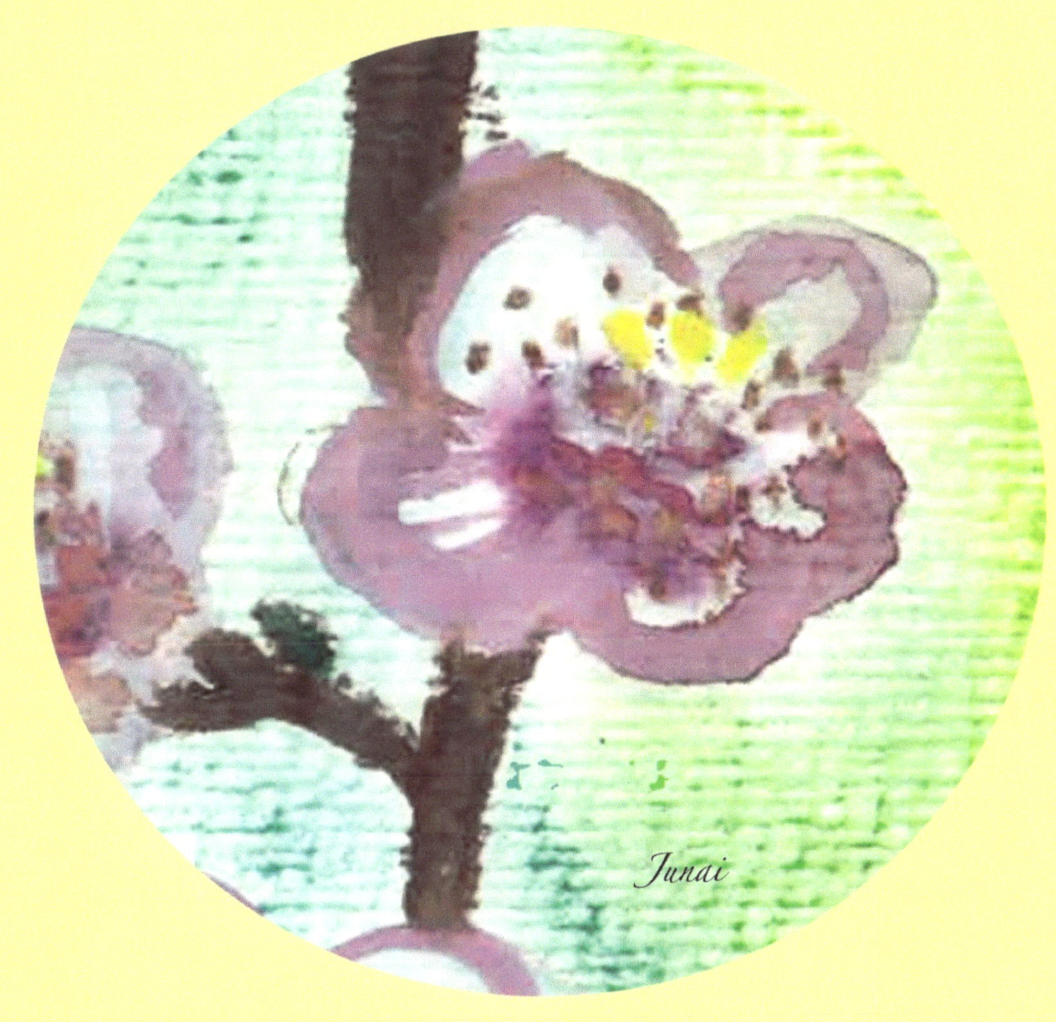

happy

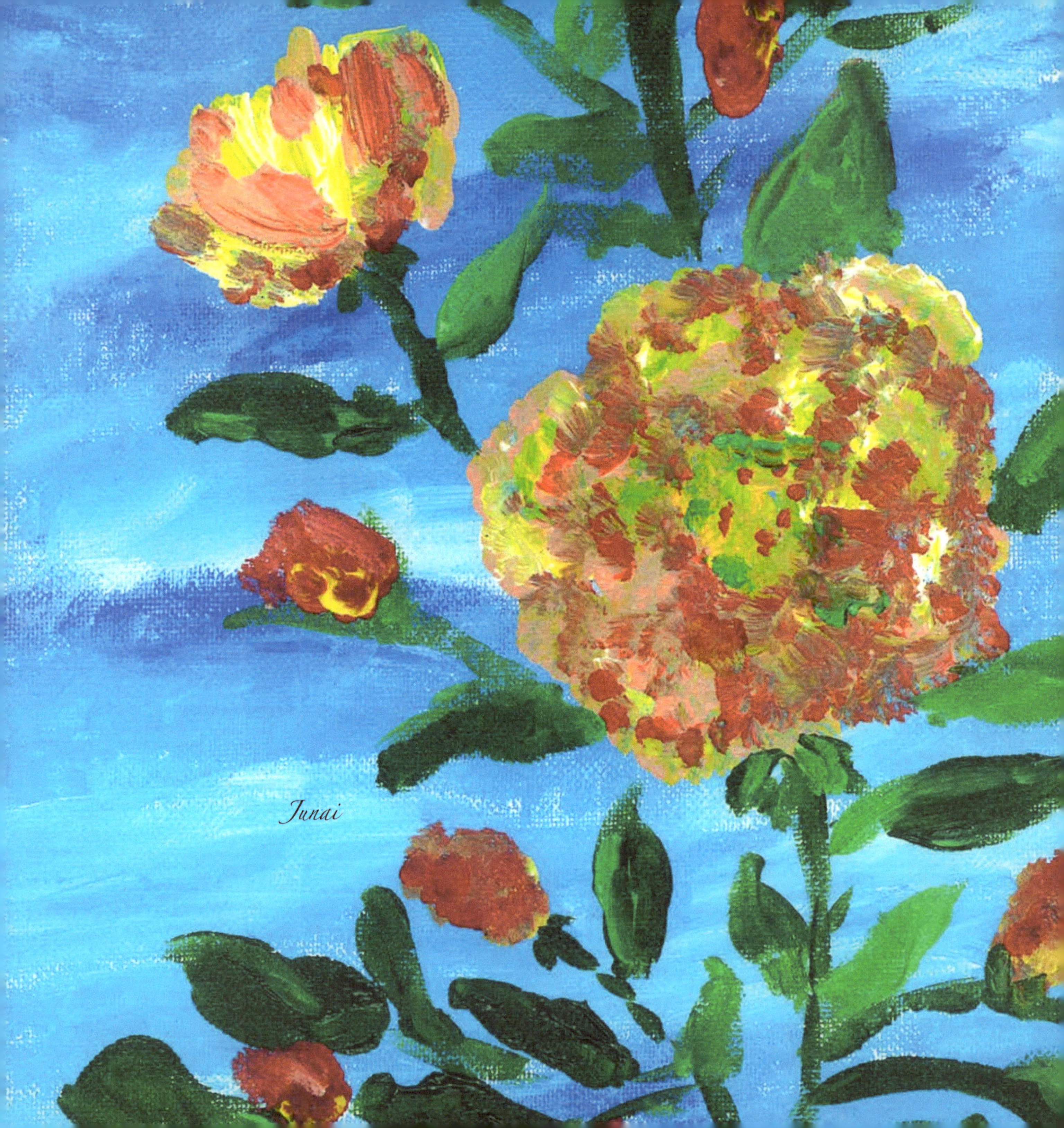
Junai

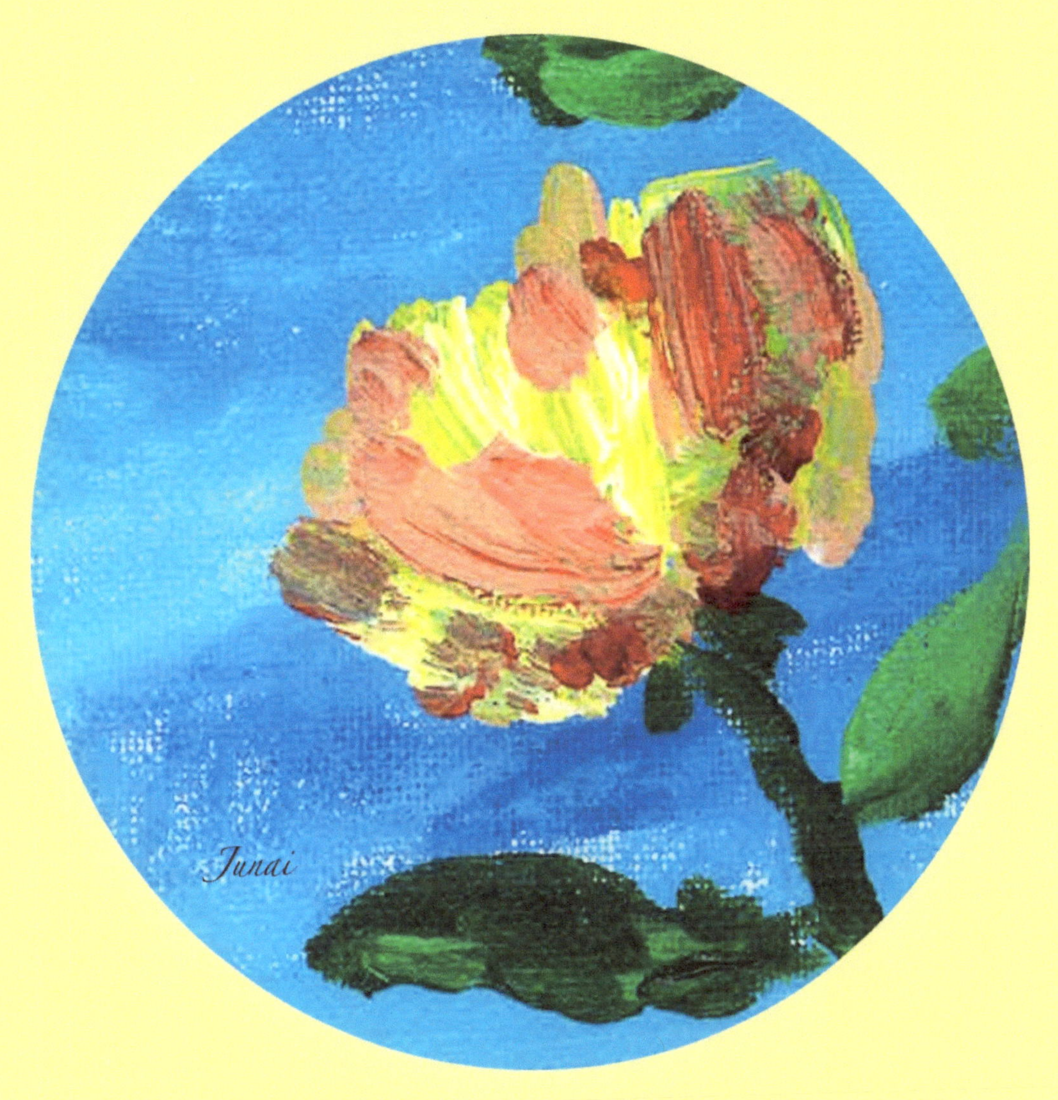

interested

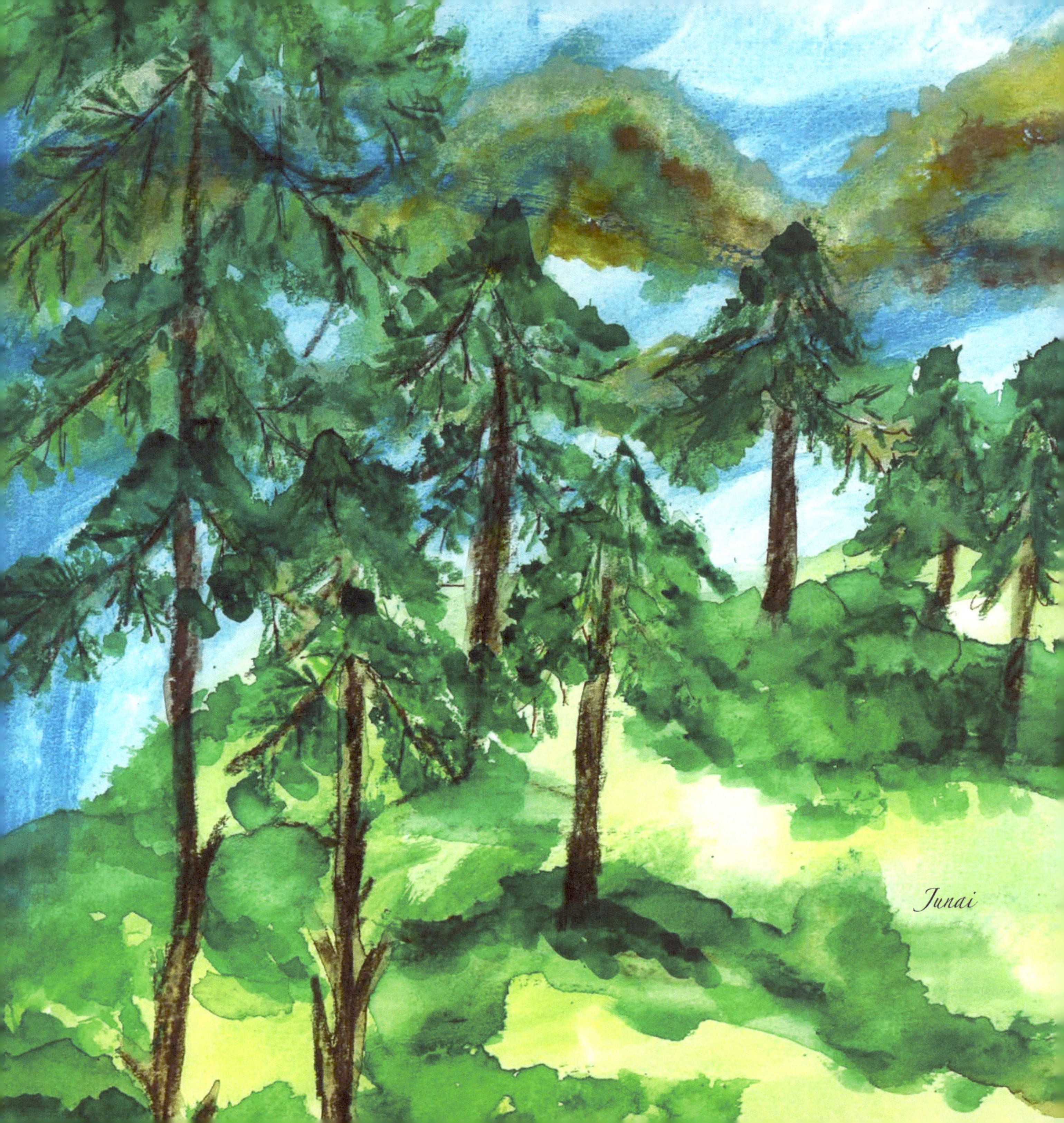
Junai

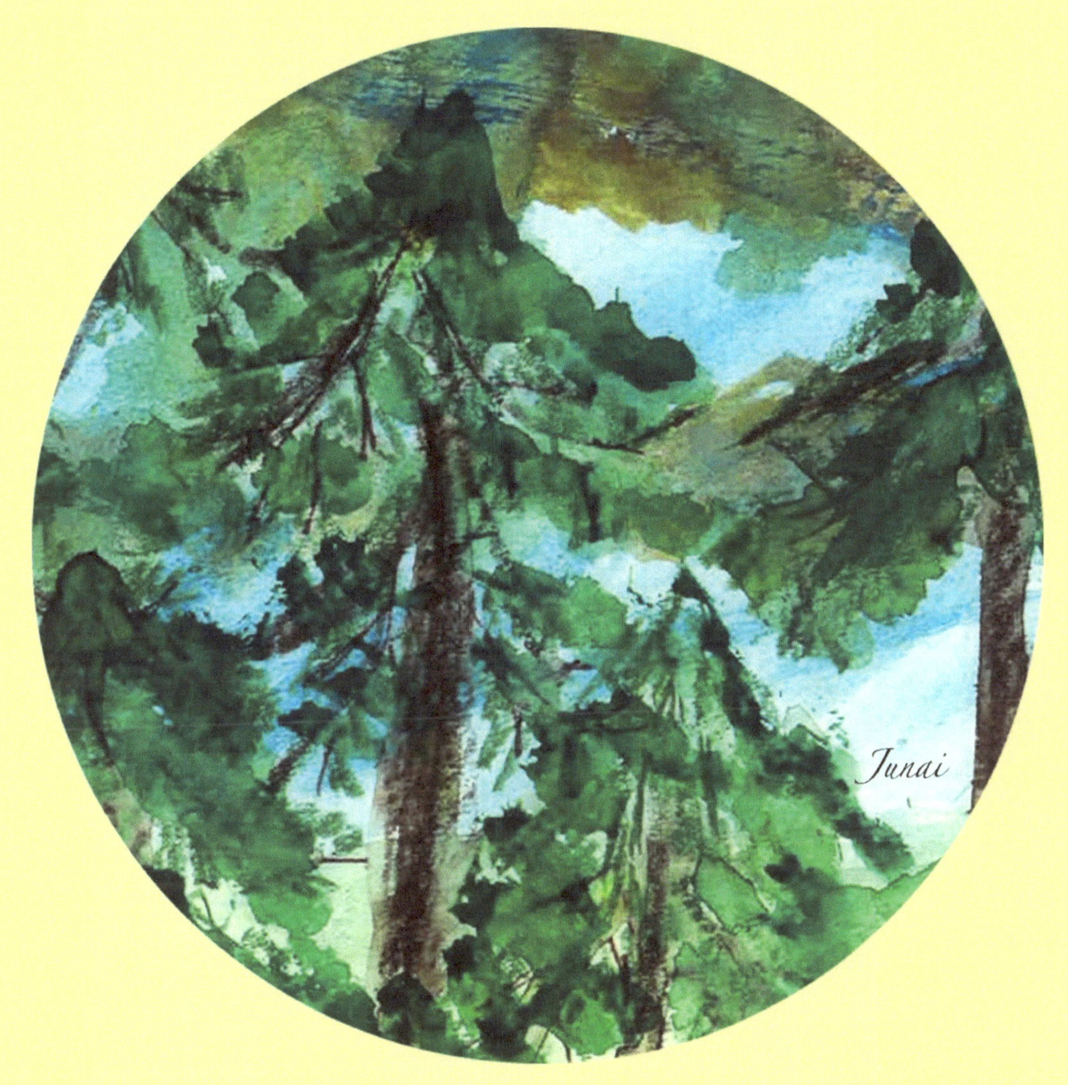

joyful

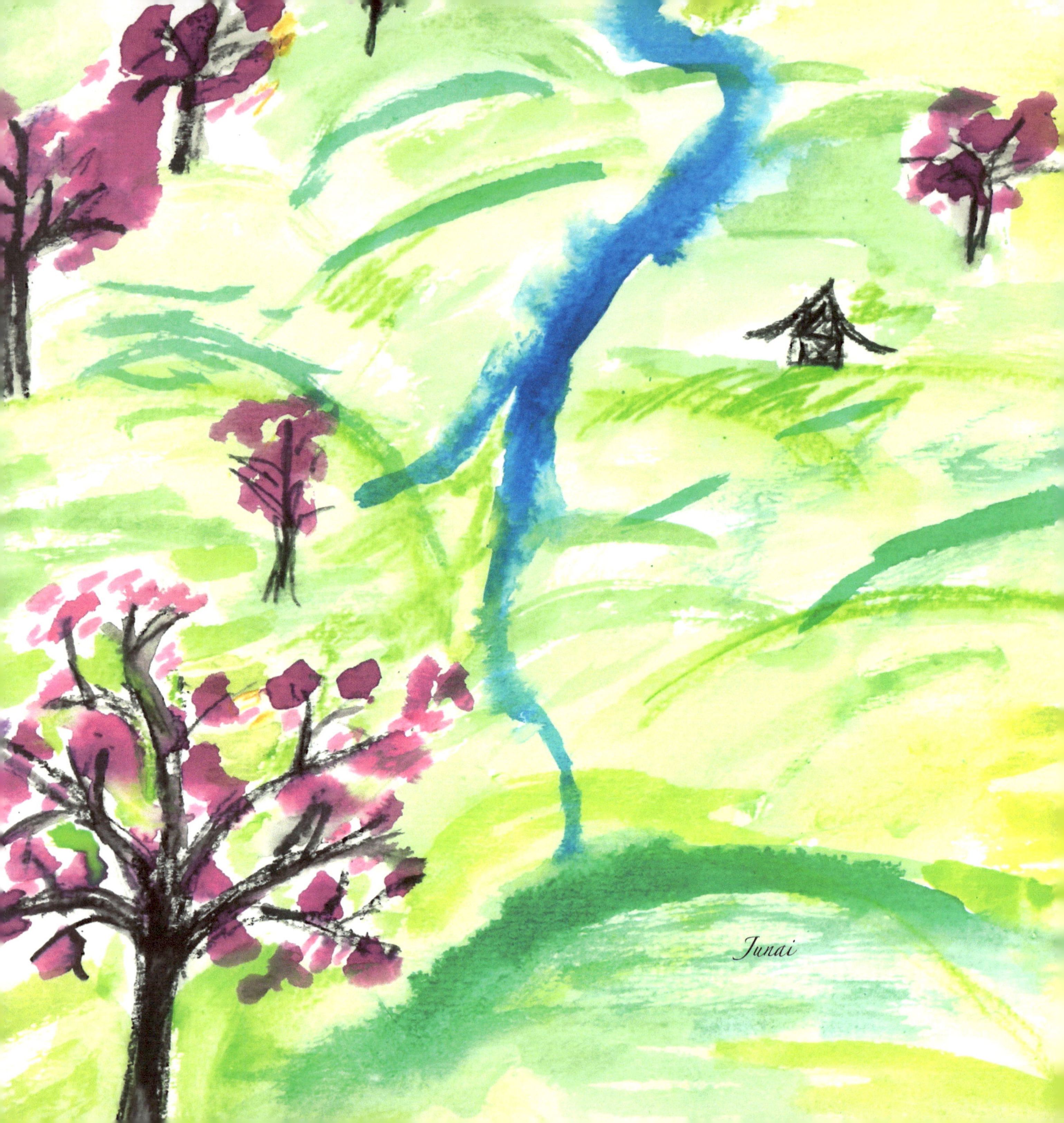
Junai

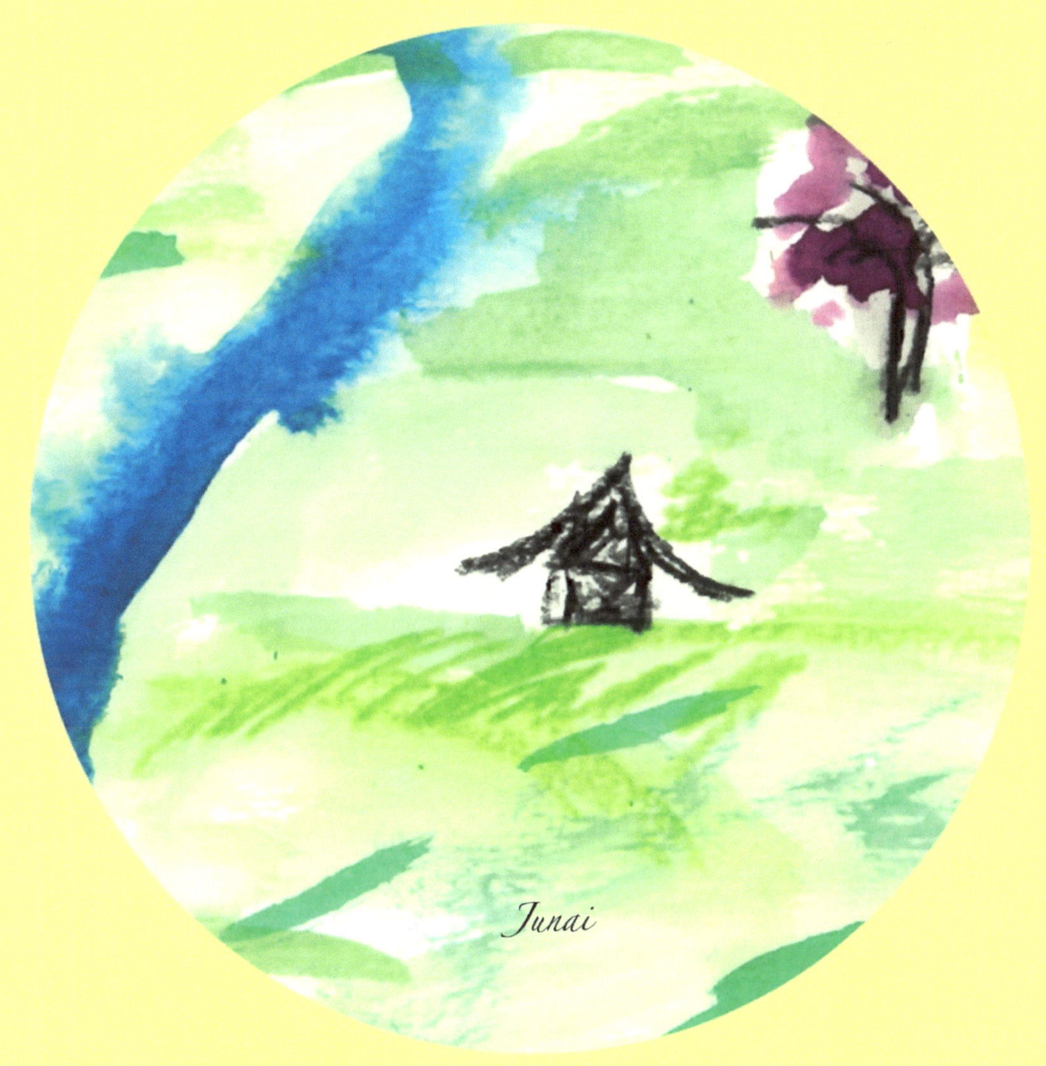

kind

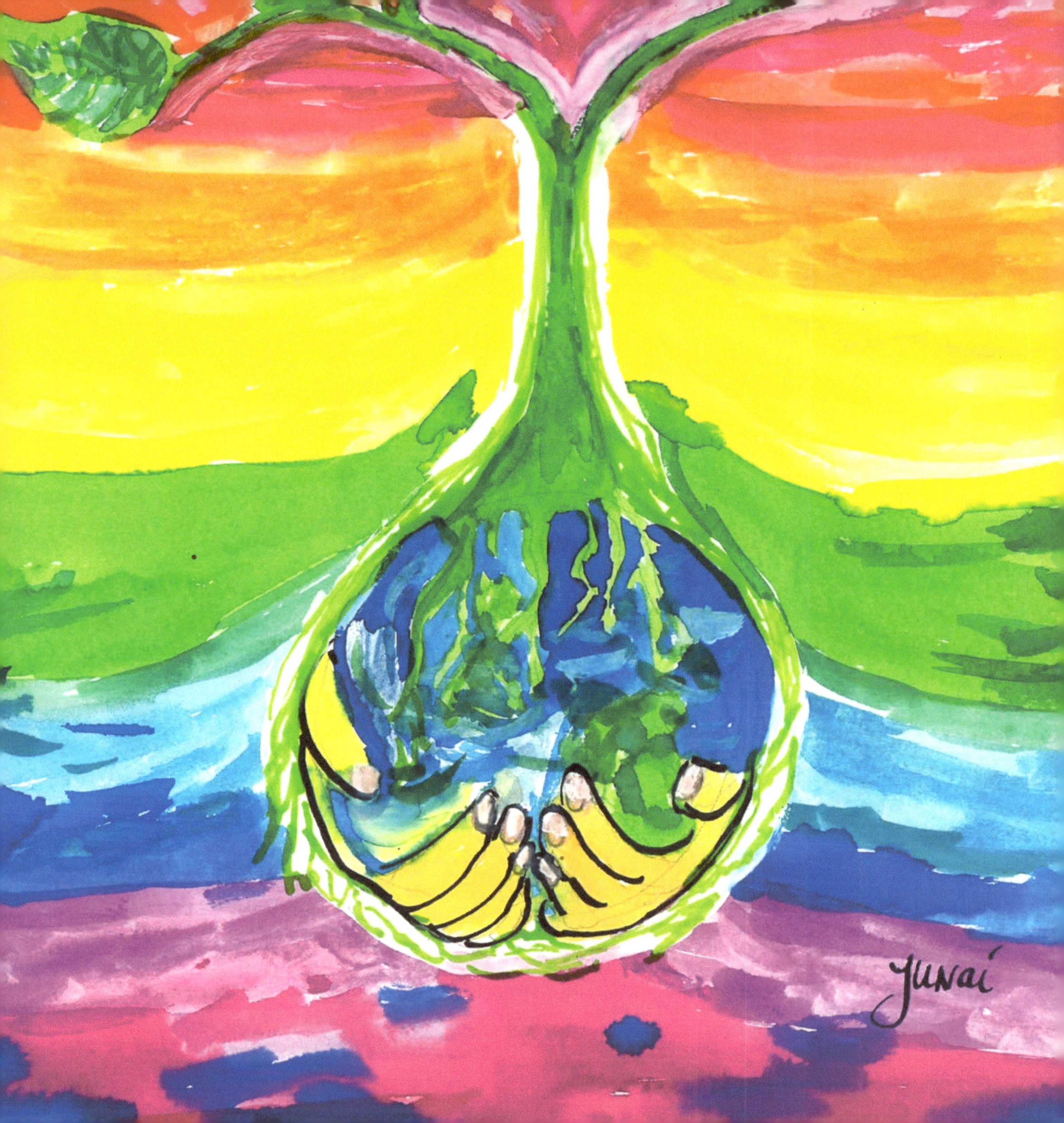
Junai

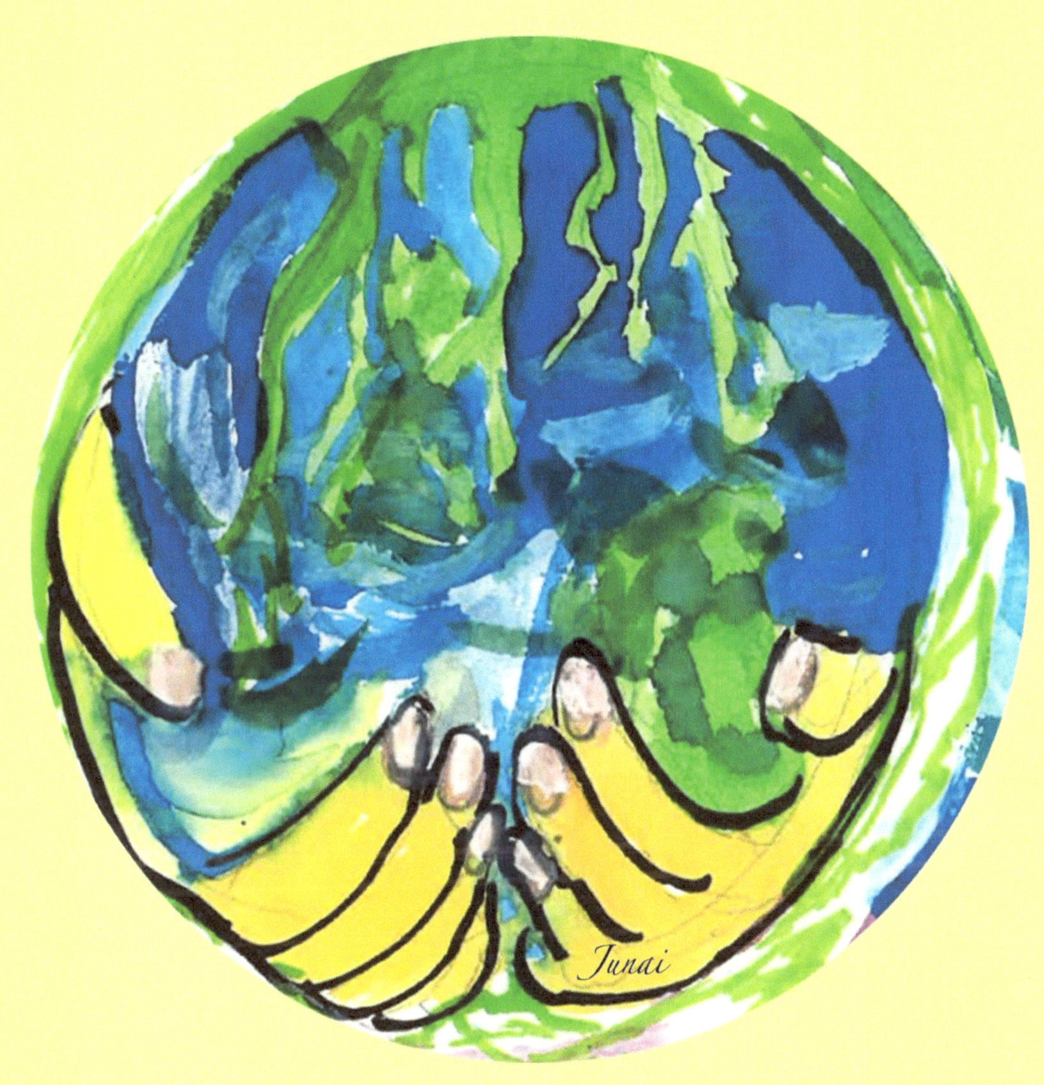

love

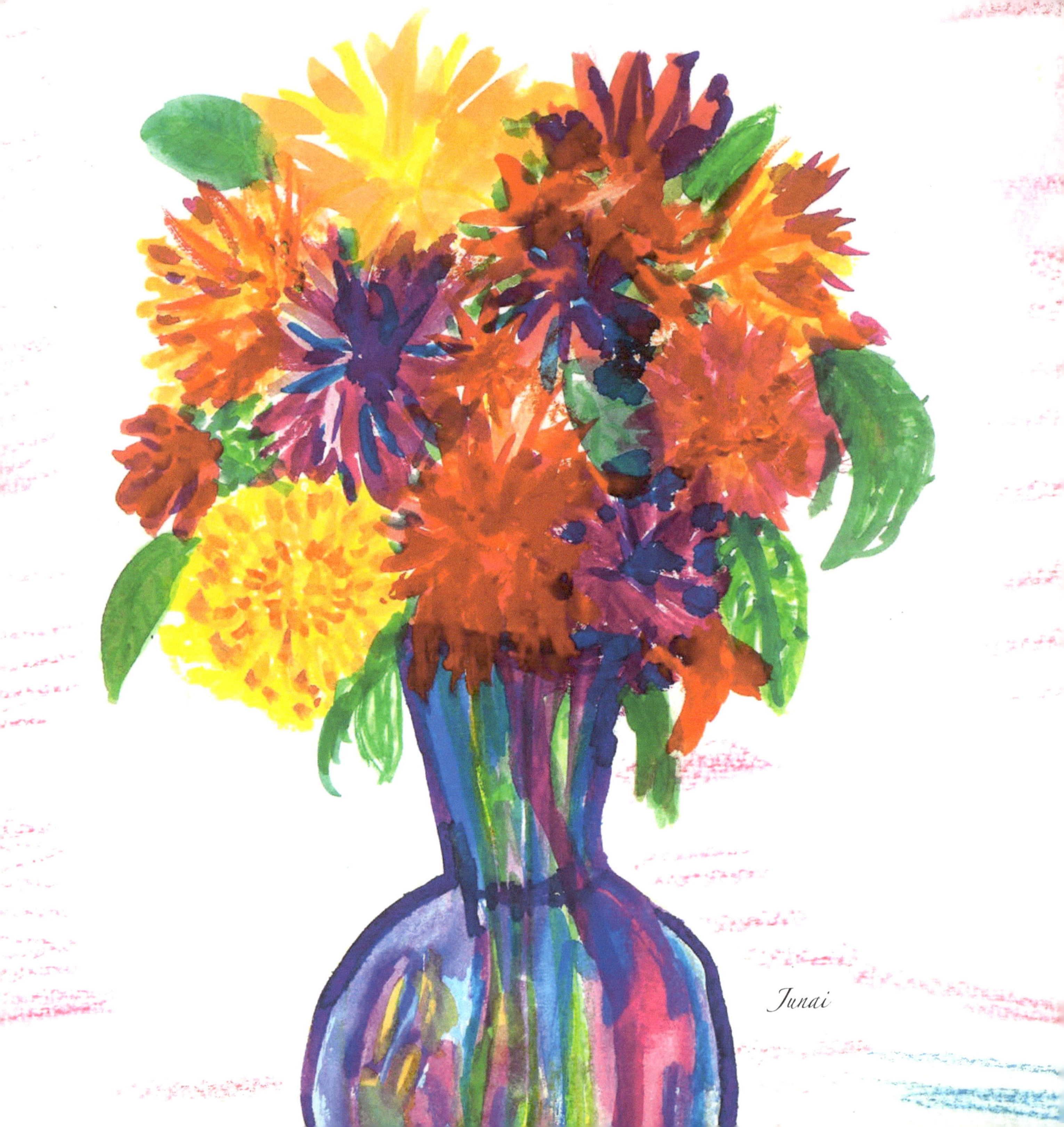
Junai

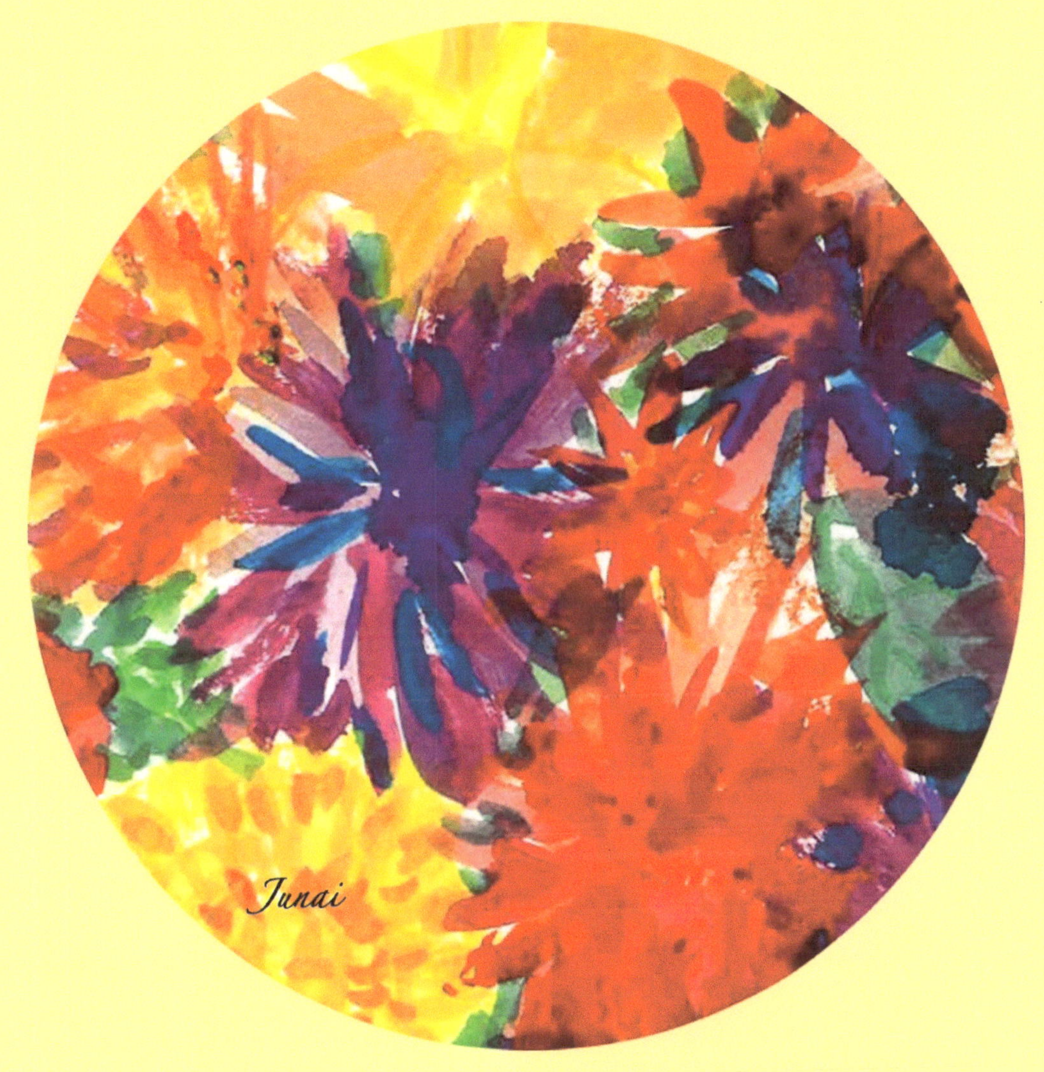

myself

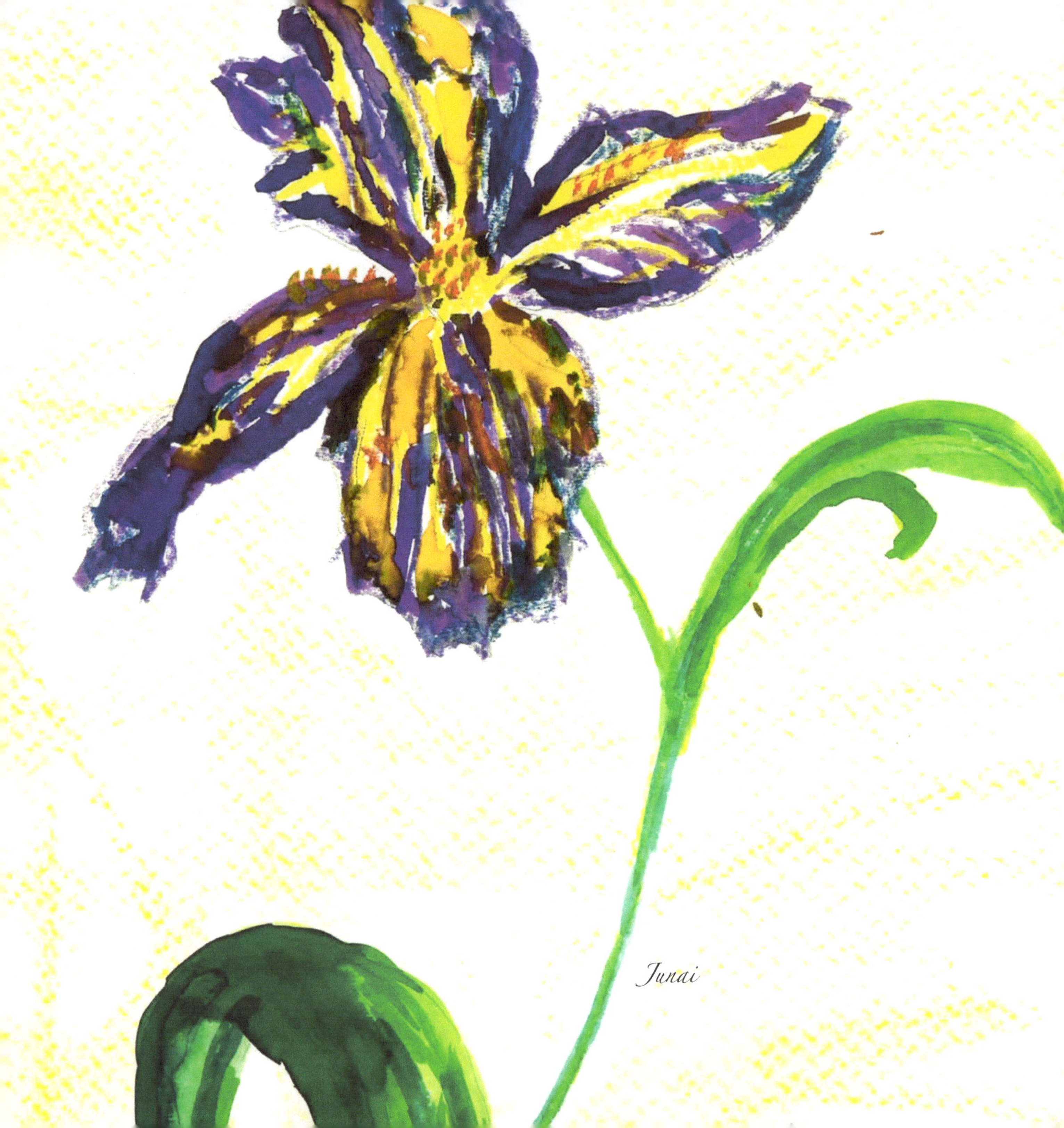
Junai

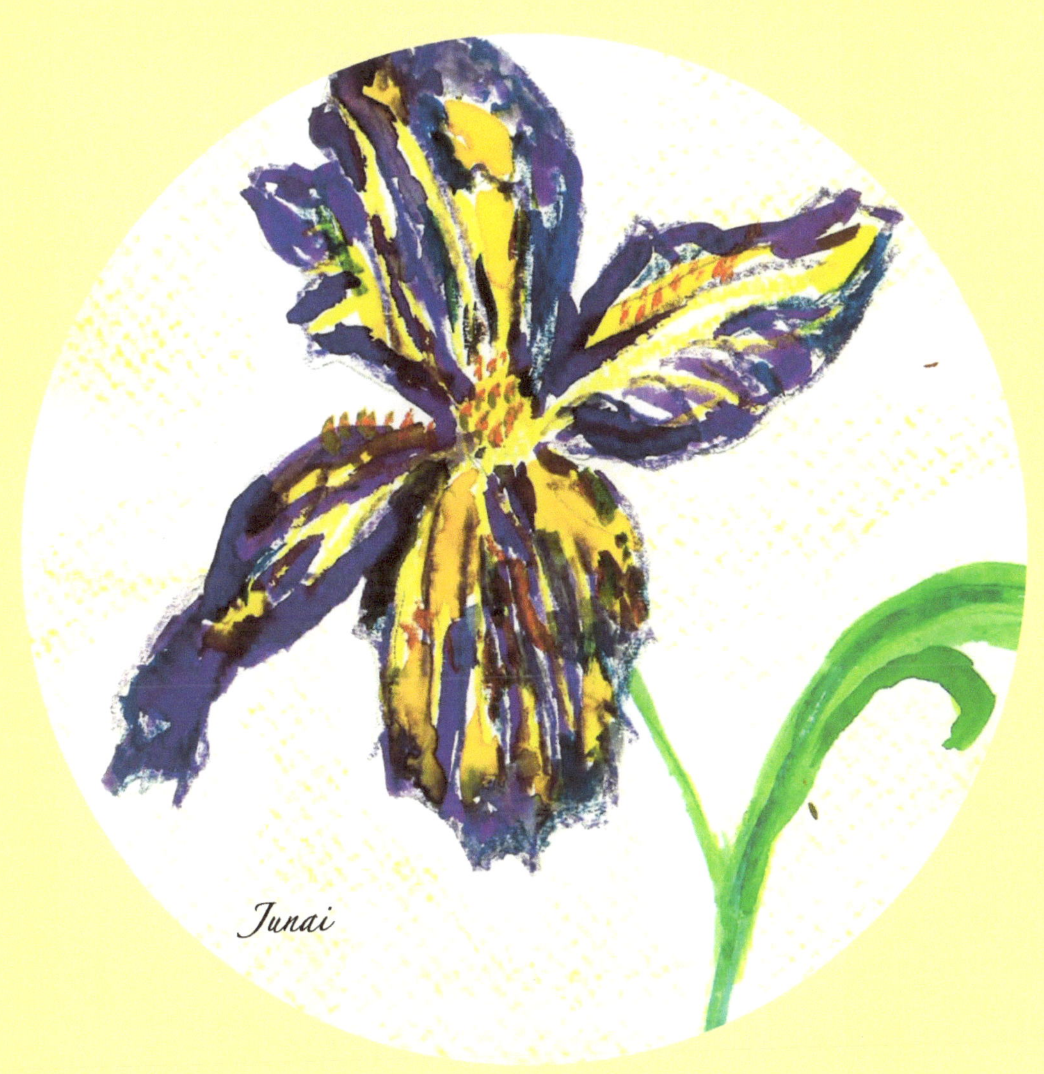

natural

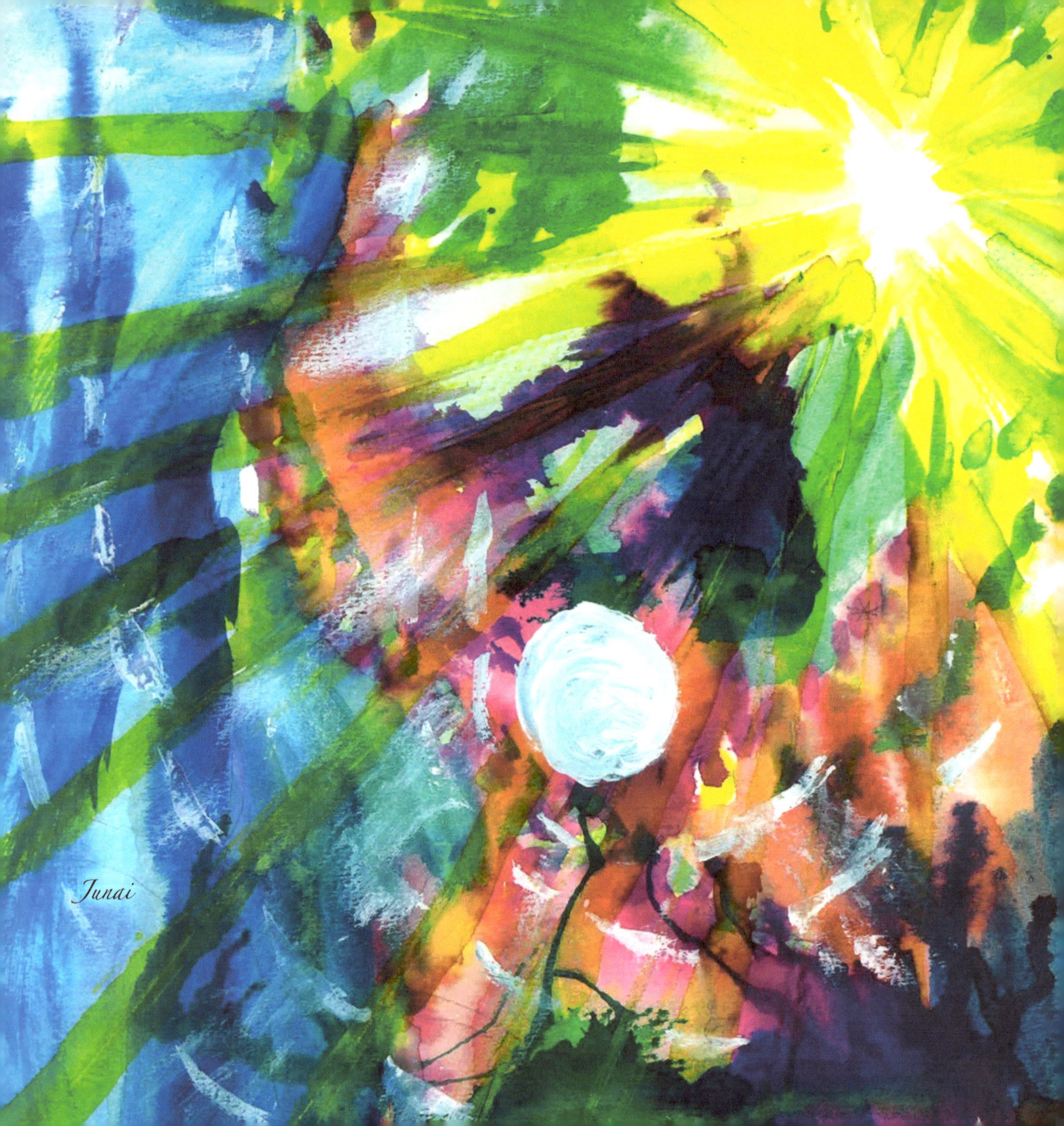
Junai

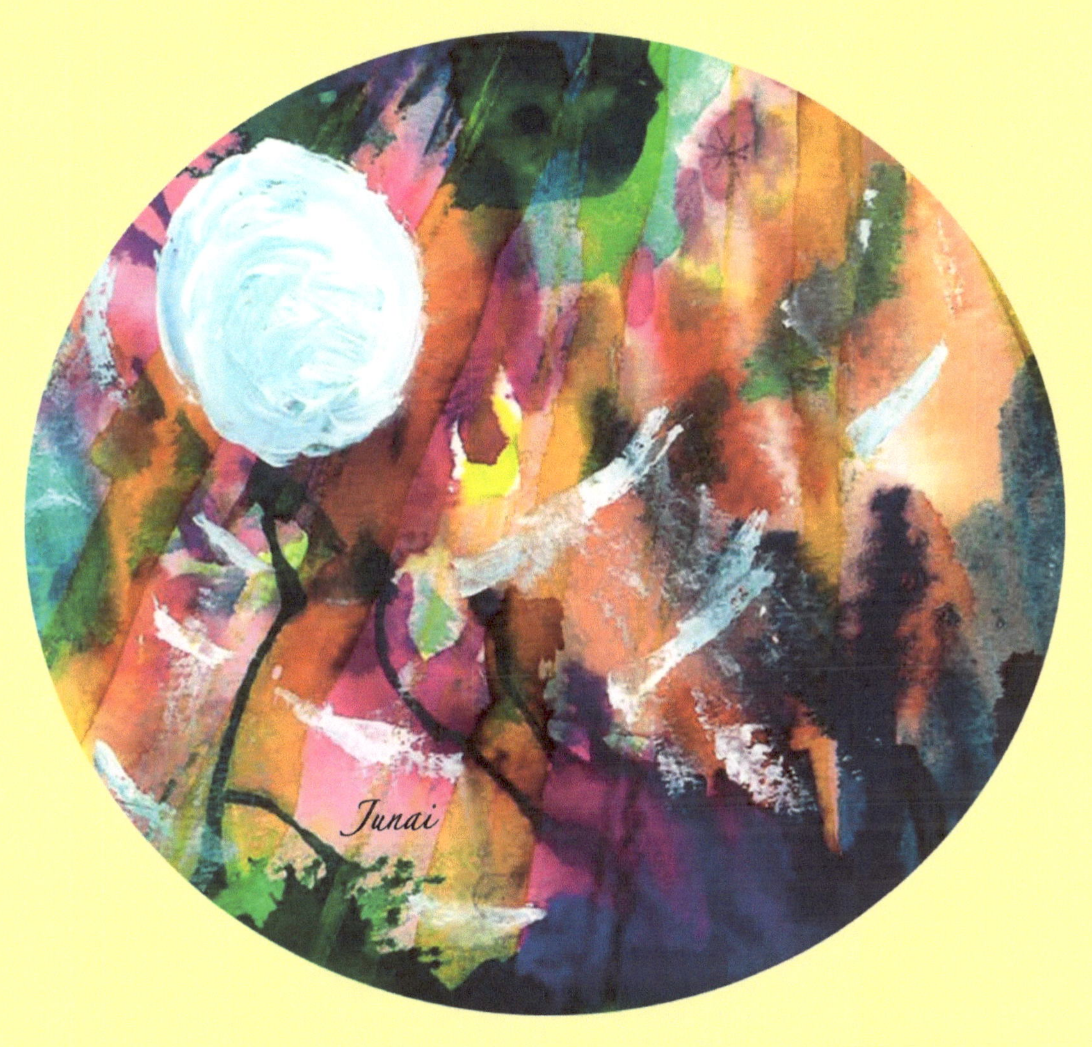

observant

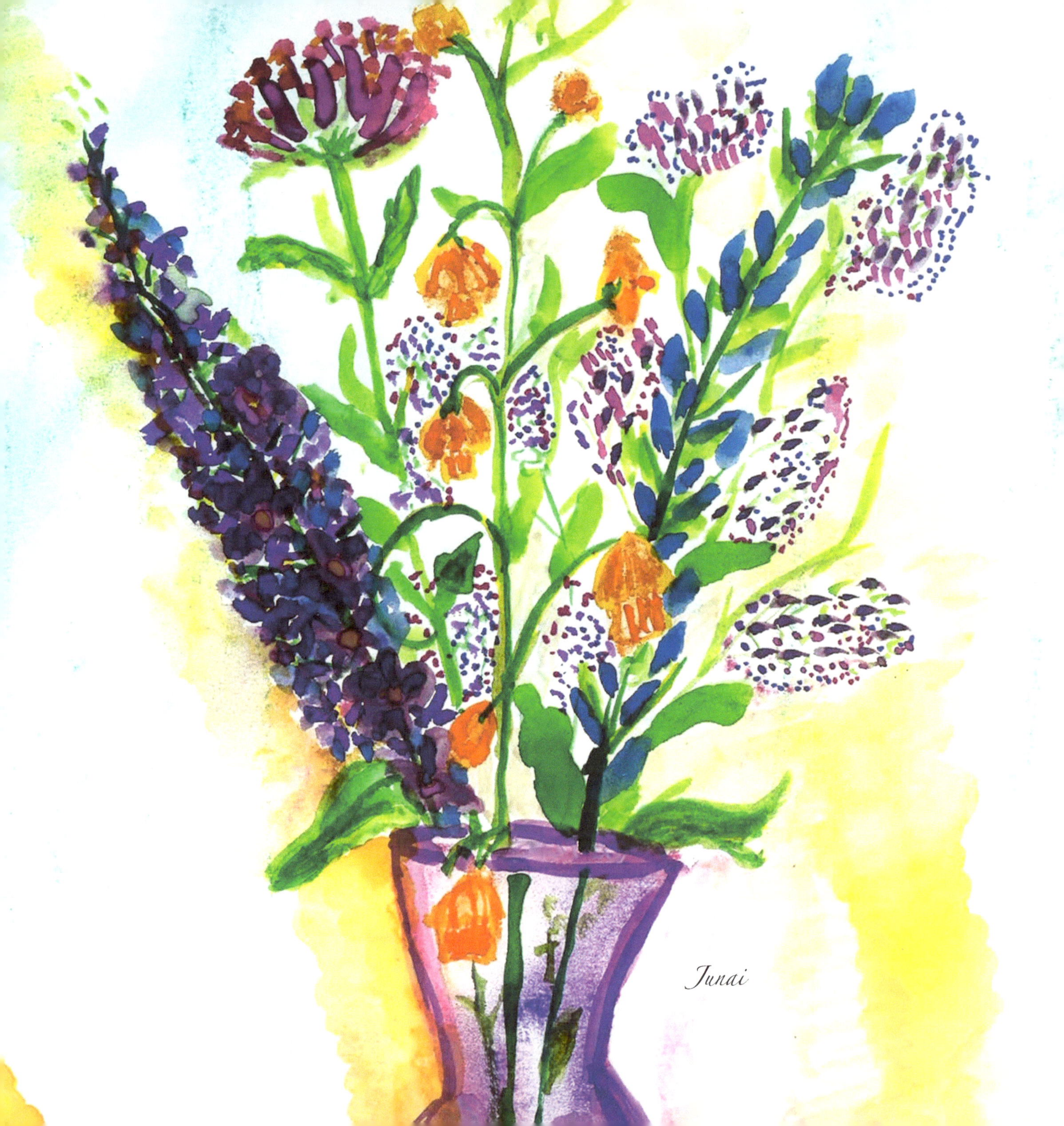
Junai

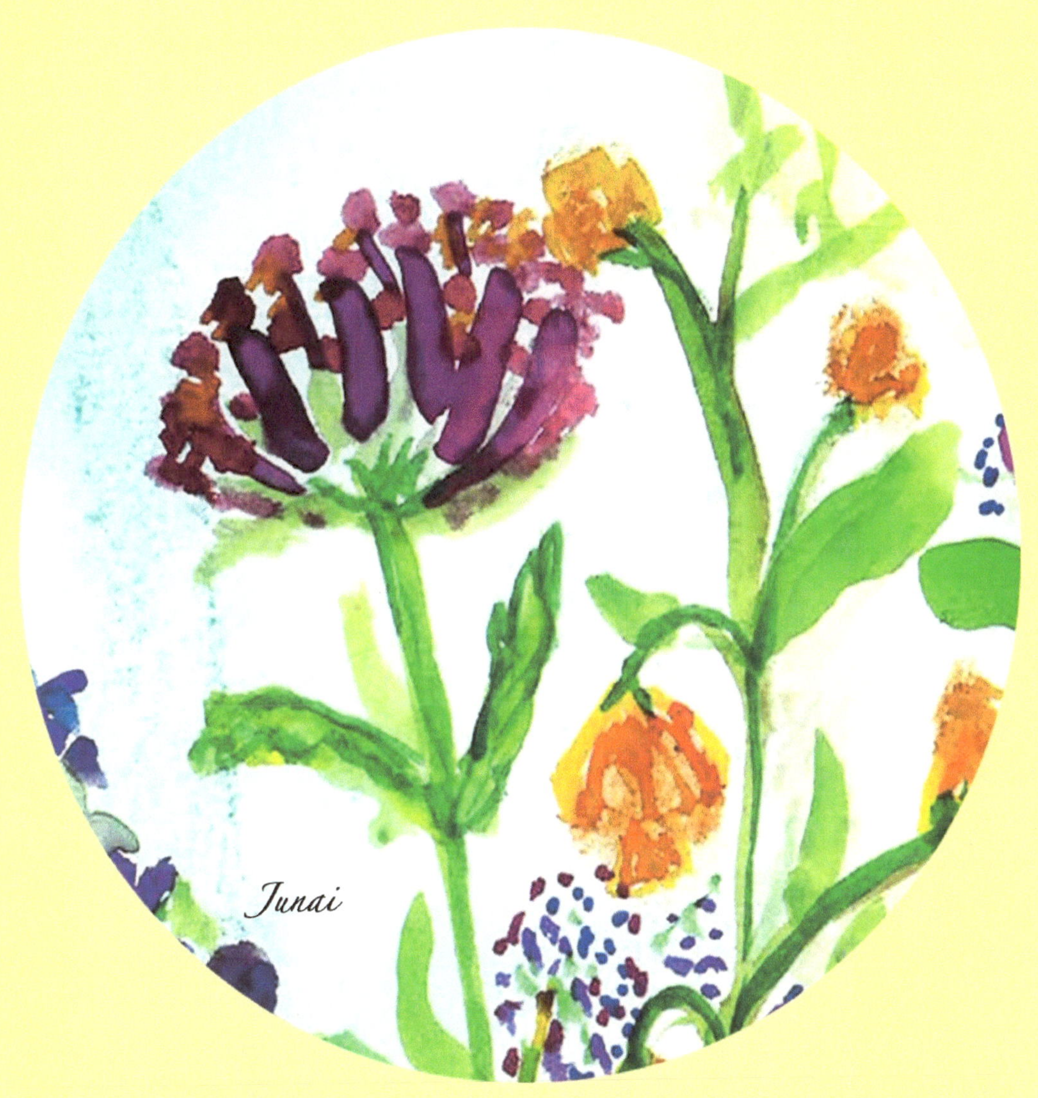

powerful

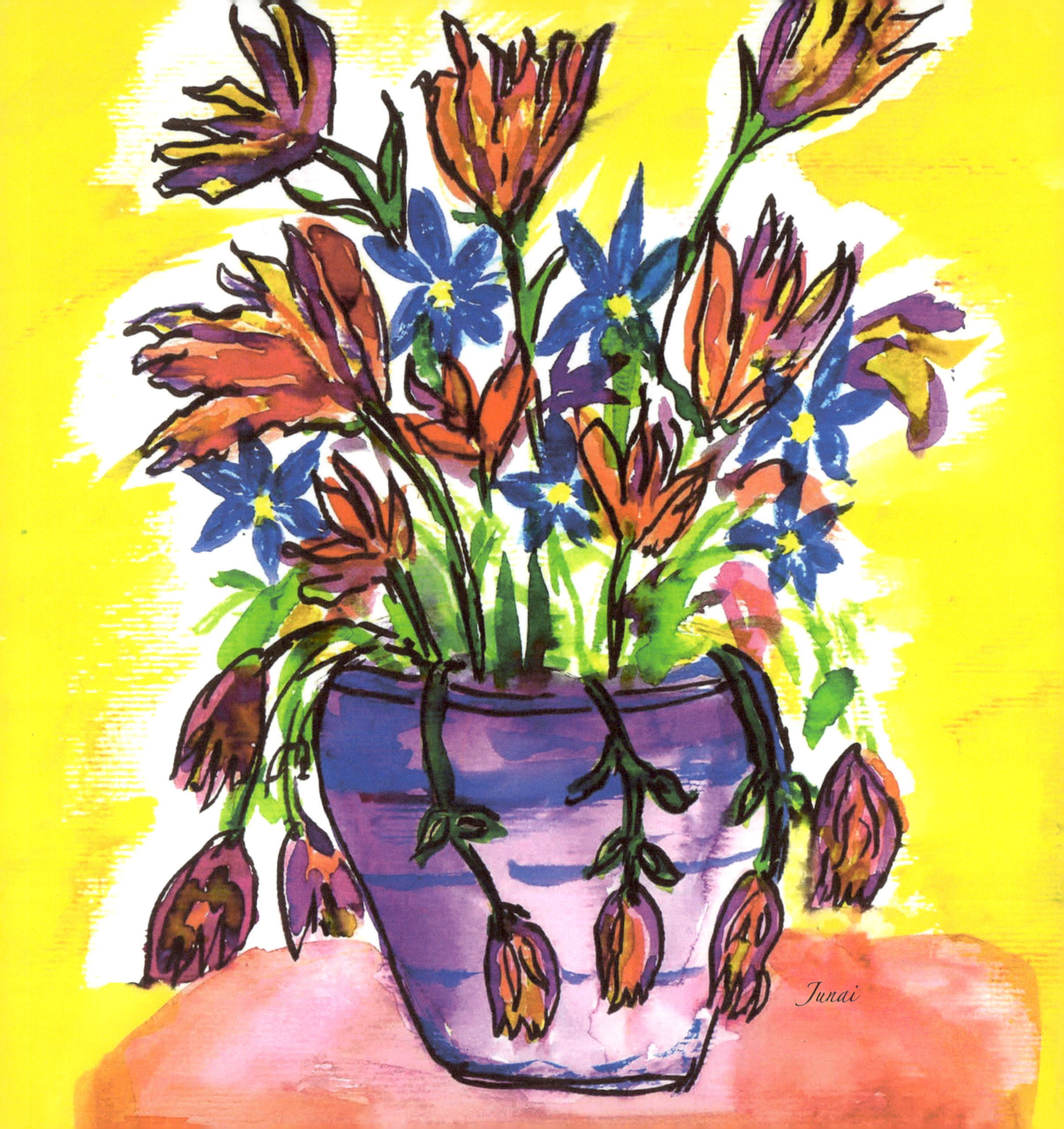
Junai

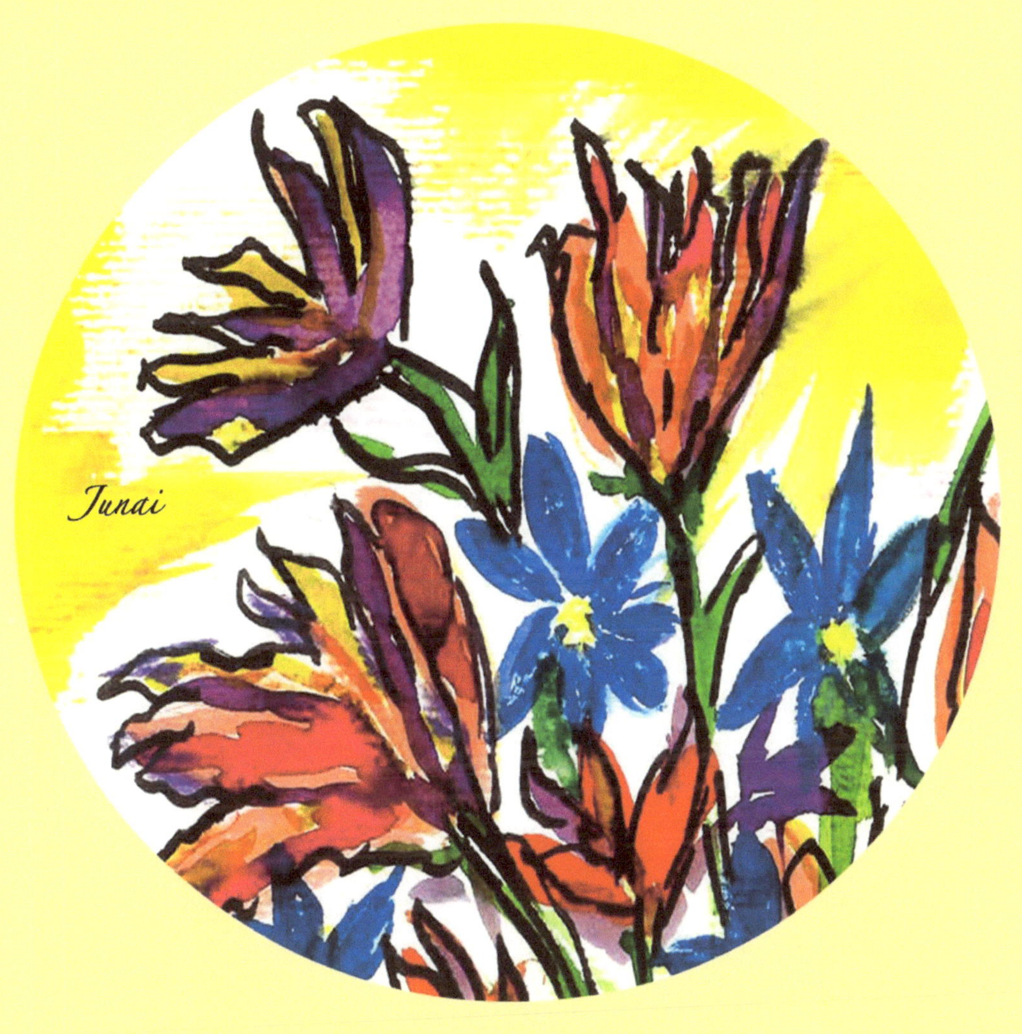

quick

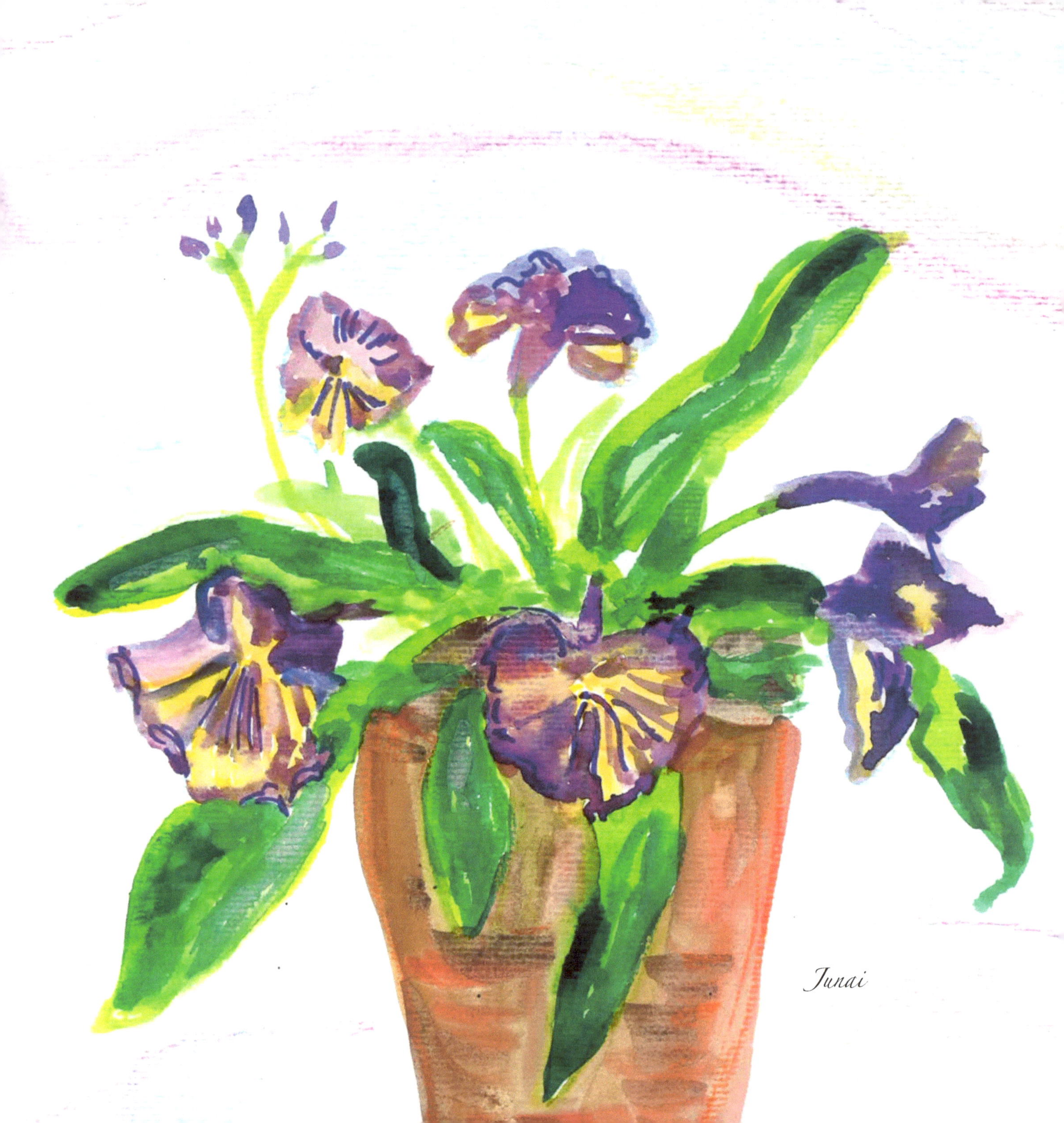
Junai

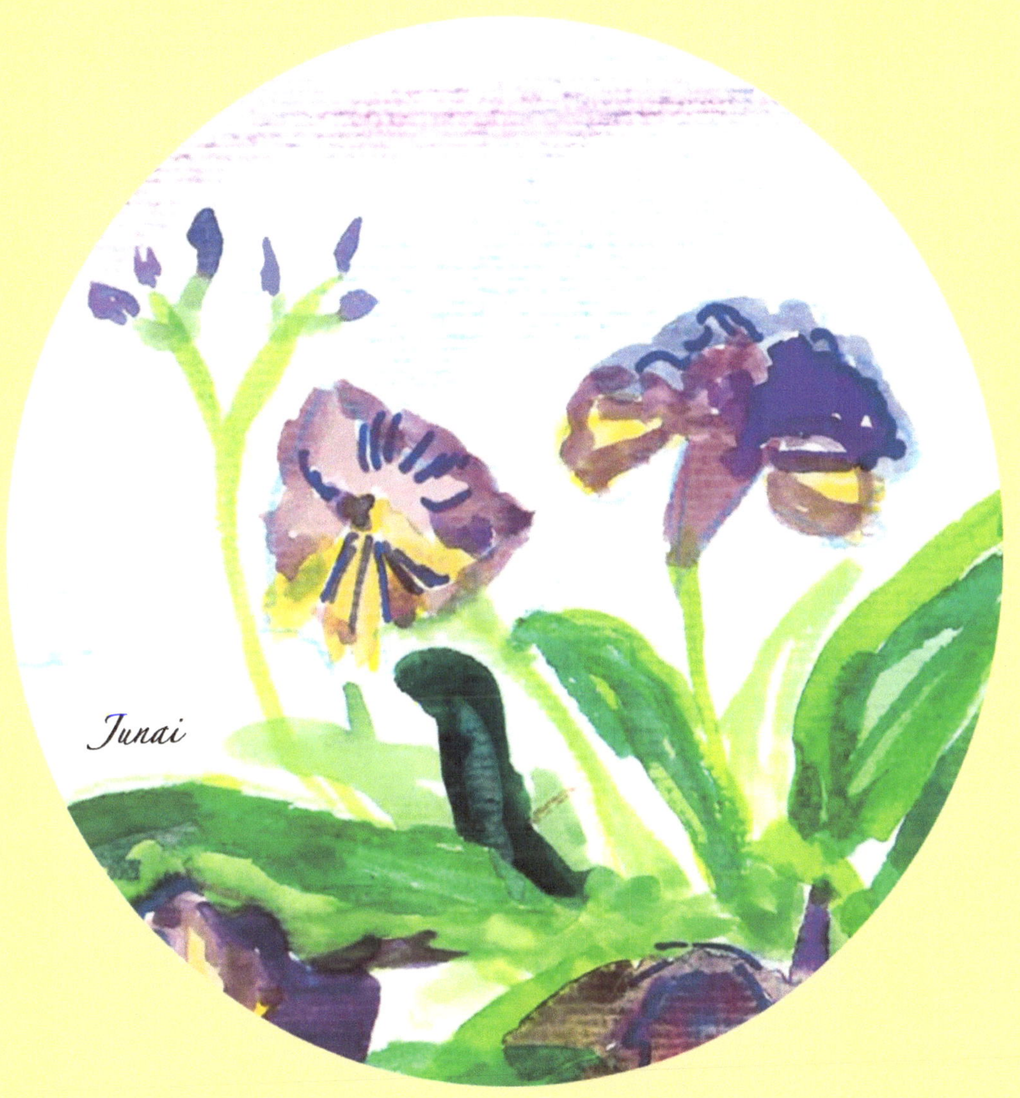

resolute

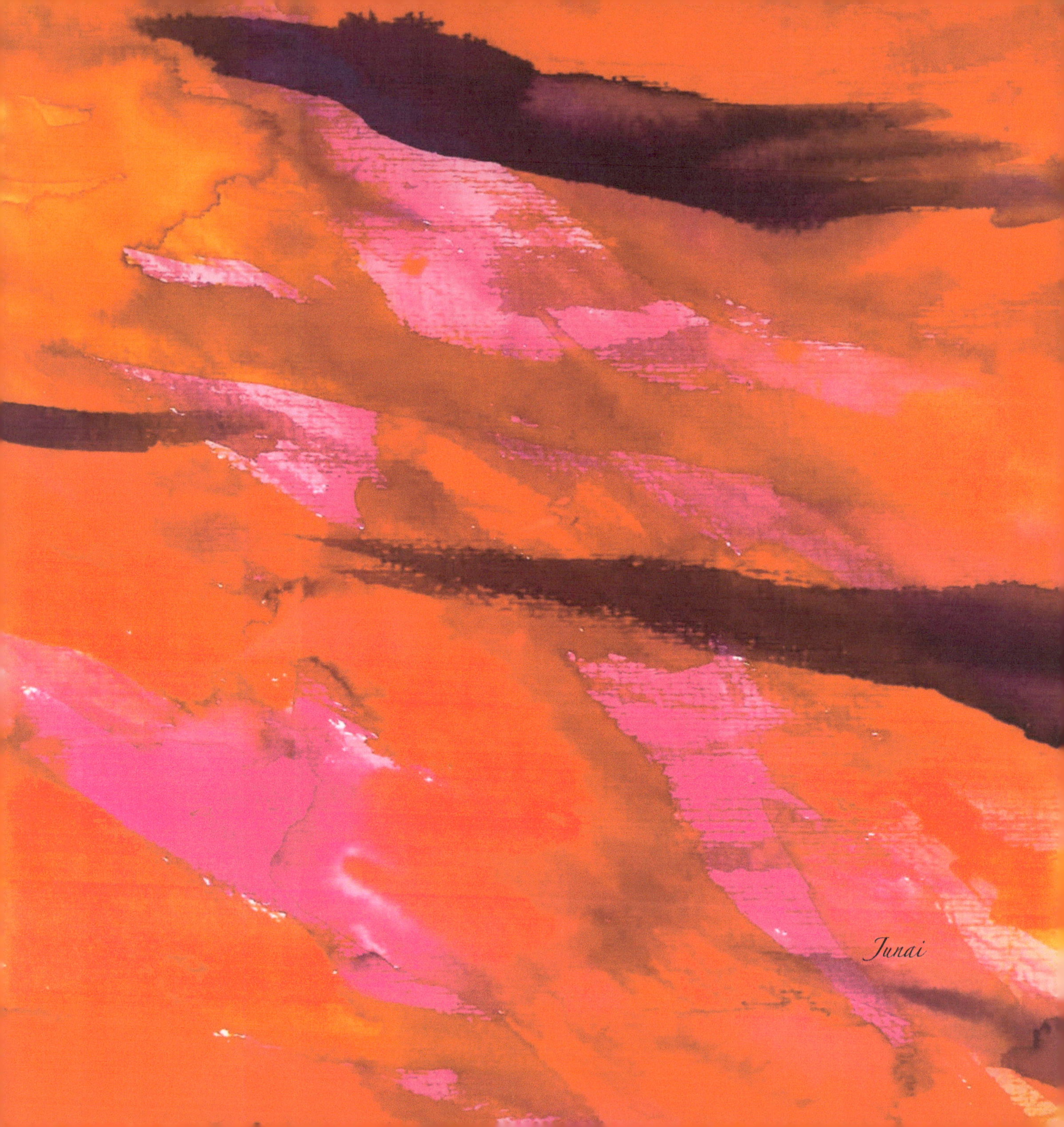
Junai

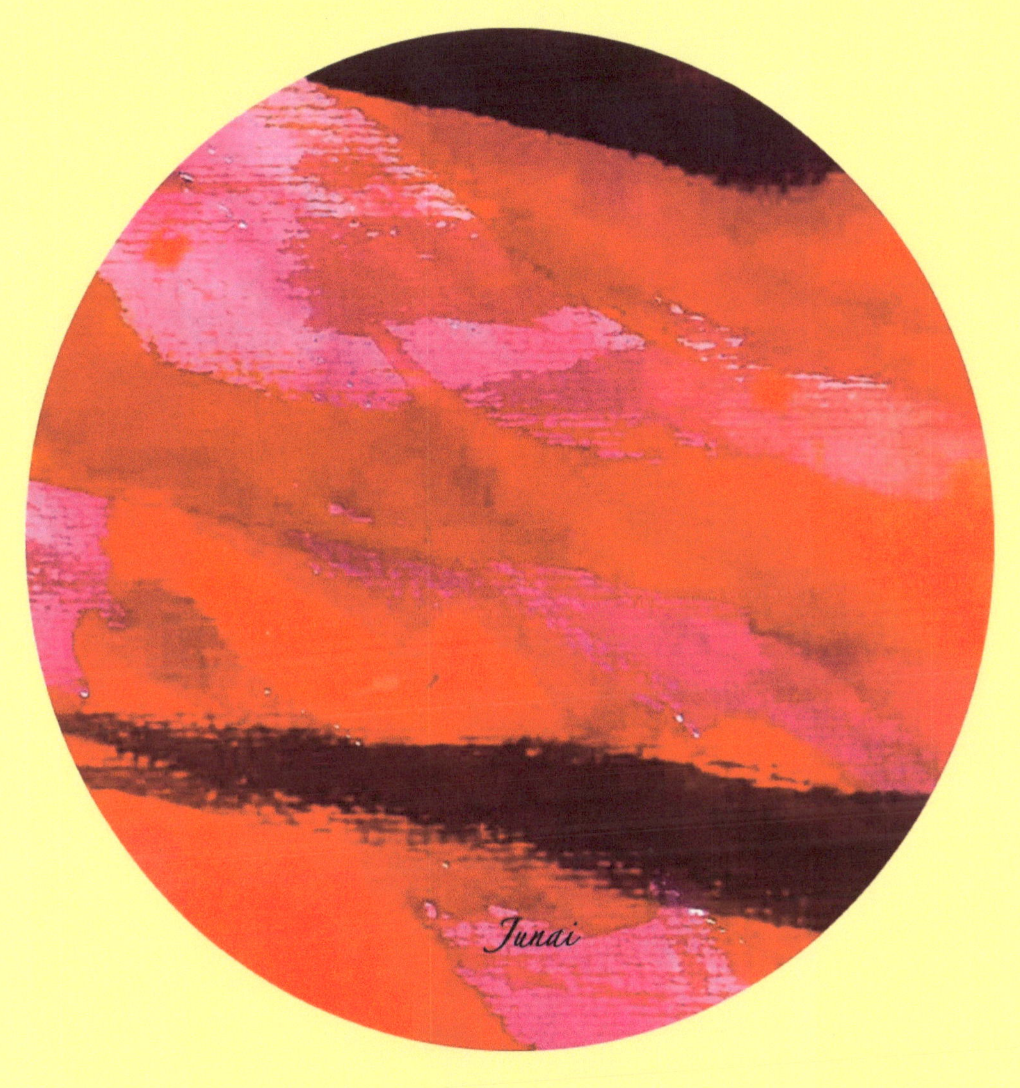

spirit

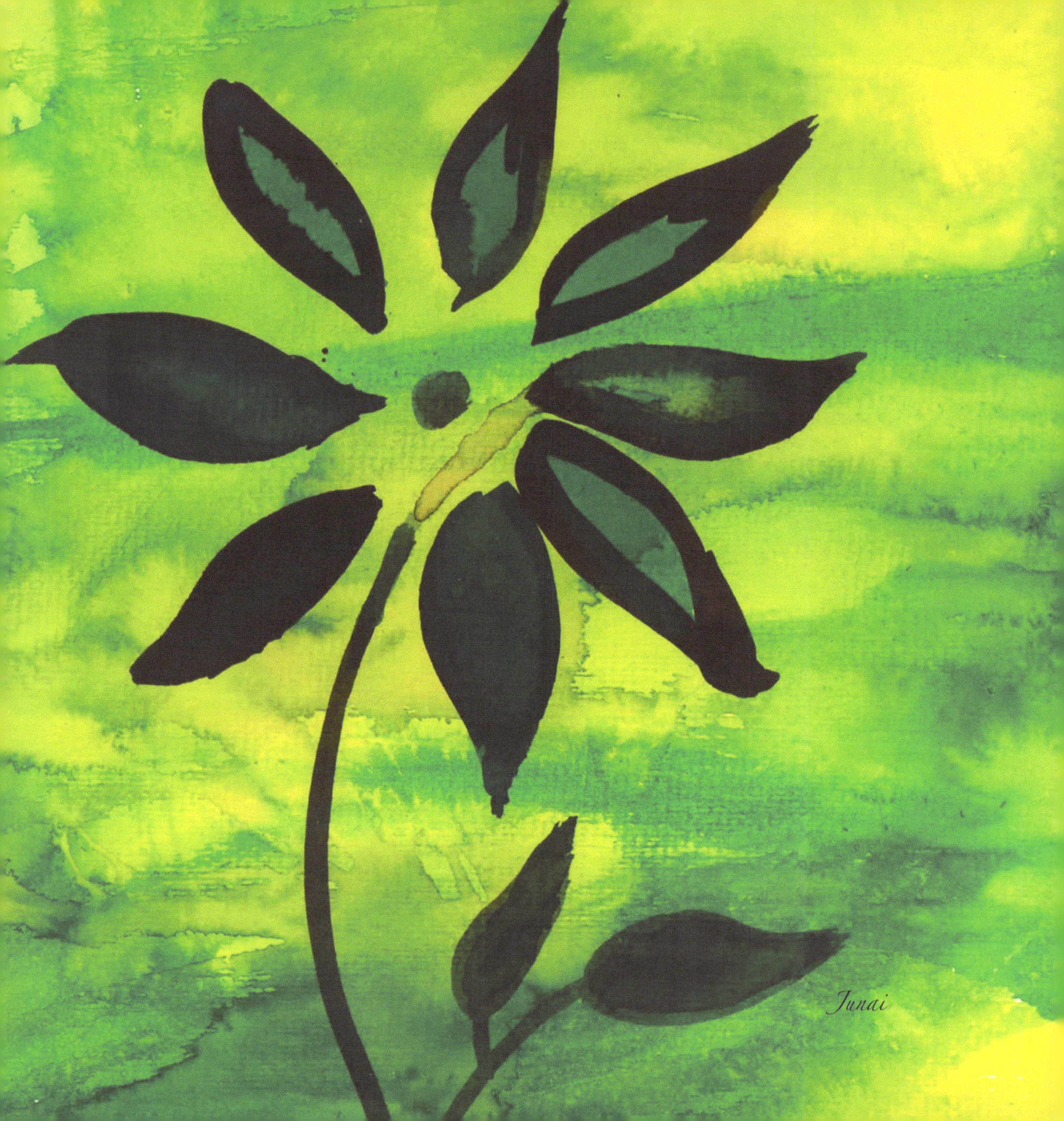
Junai

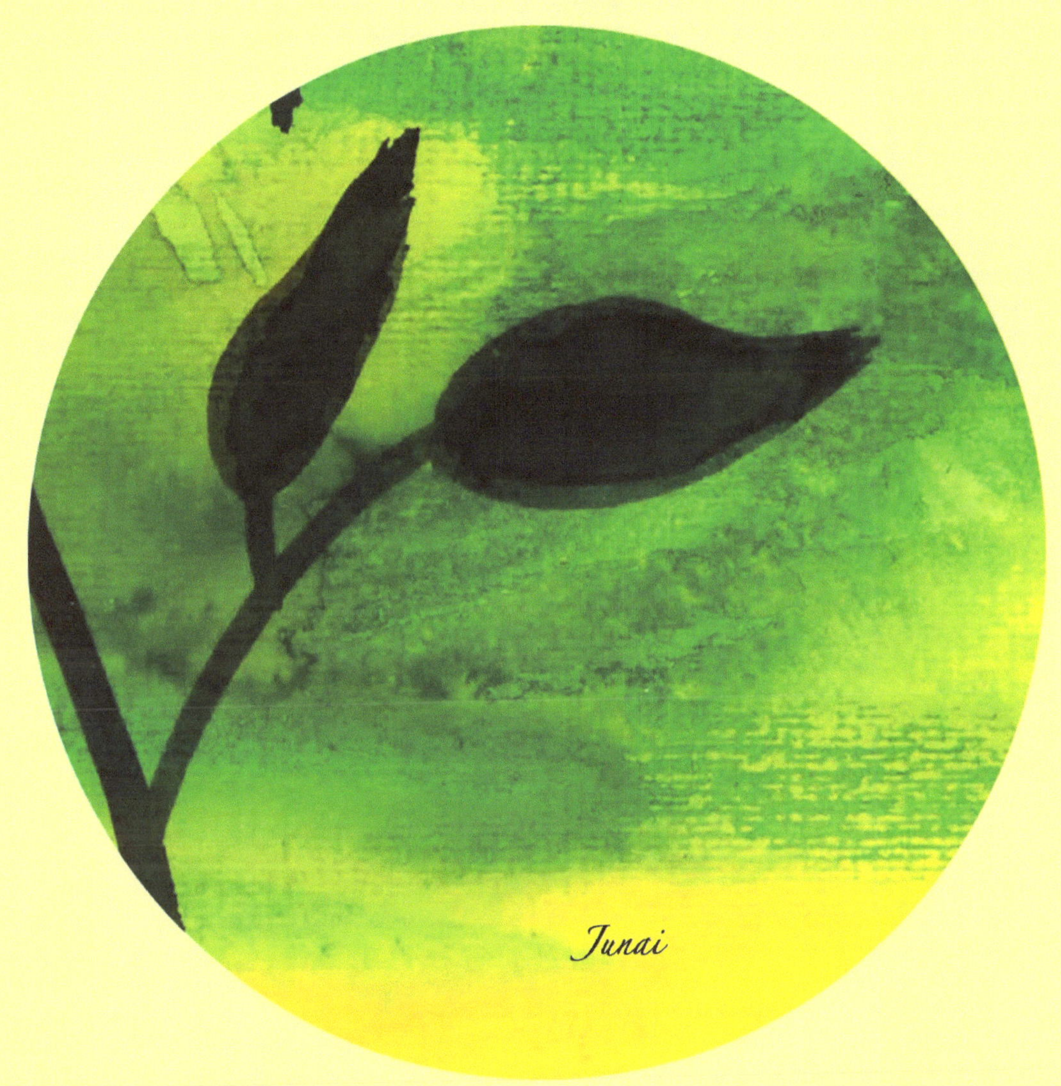

tolerant

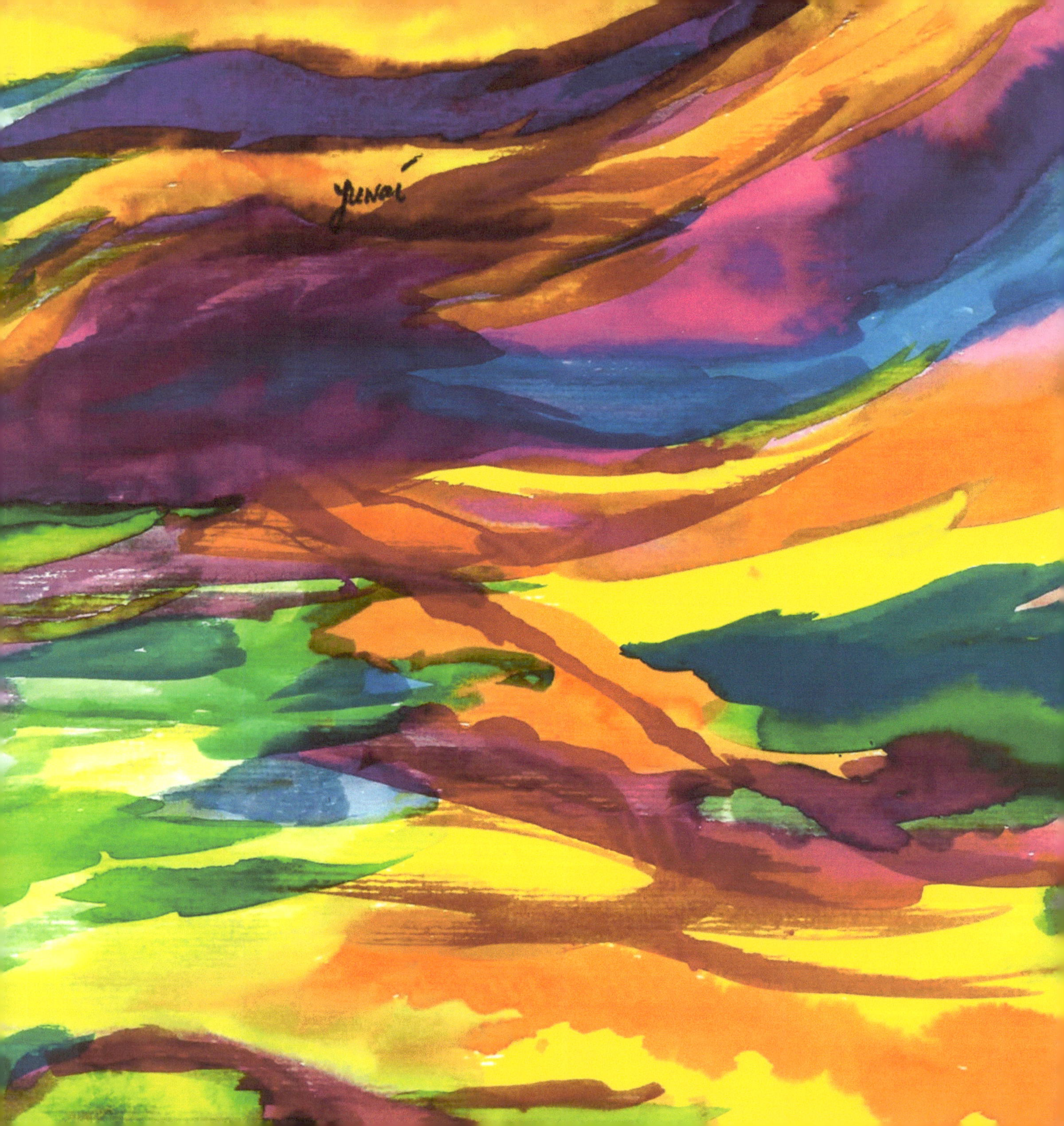

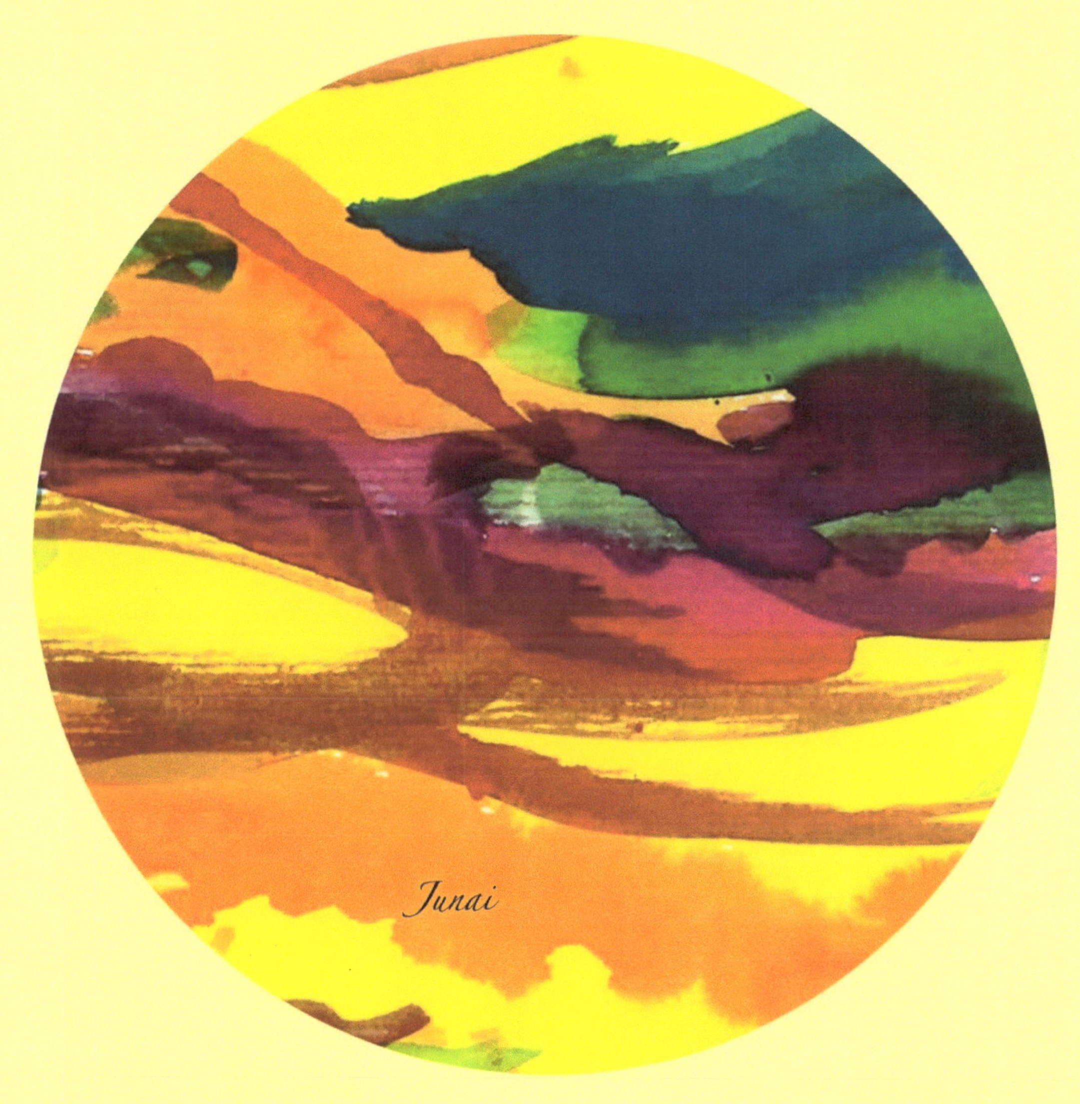

unique

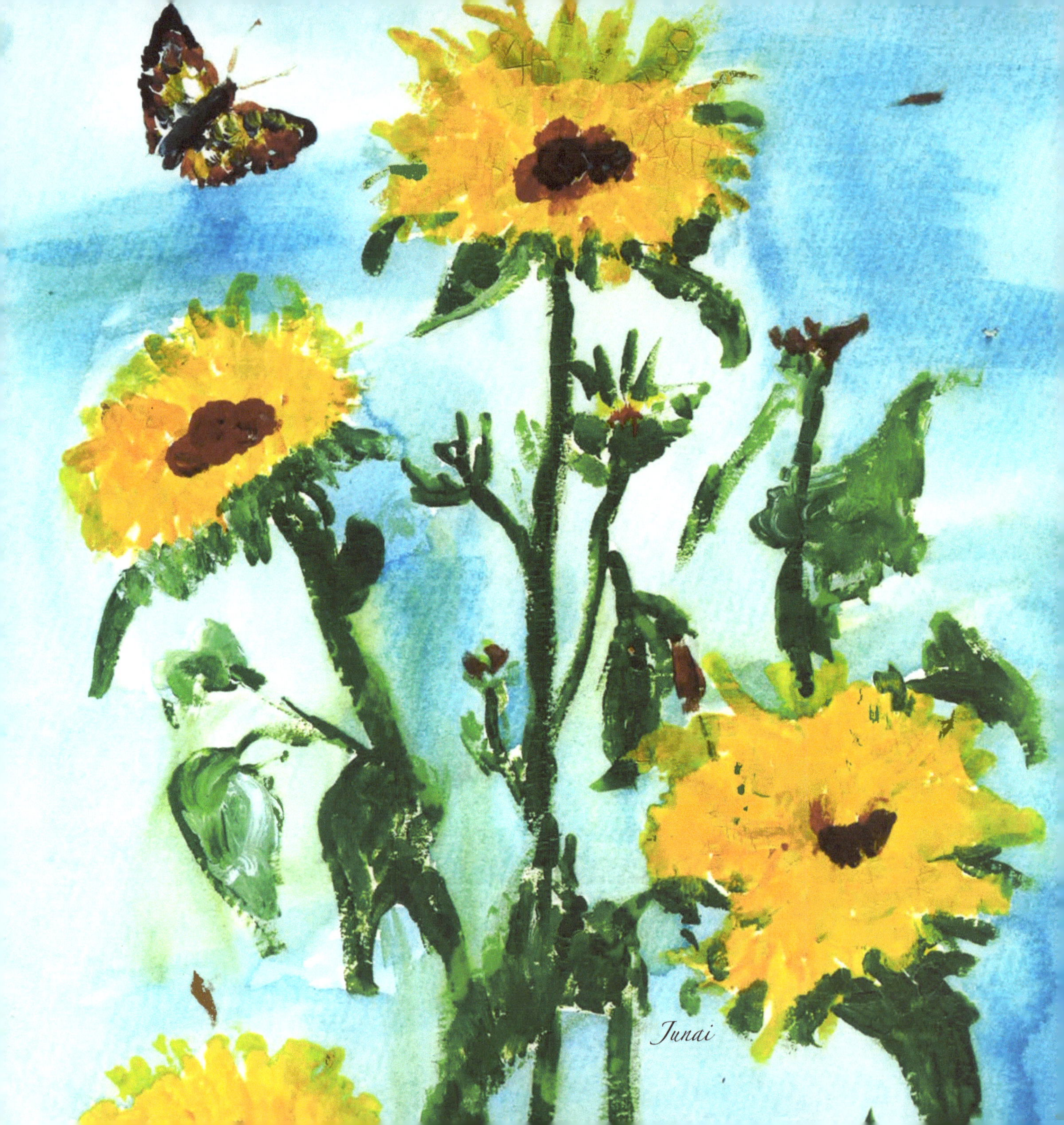
Junai

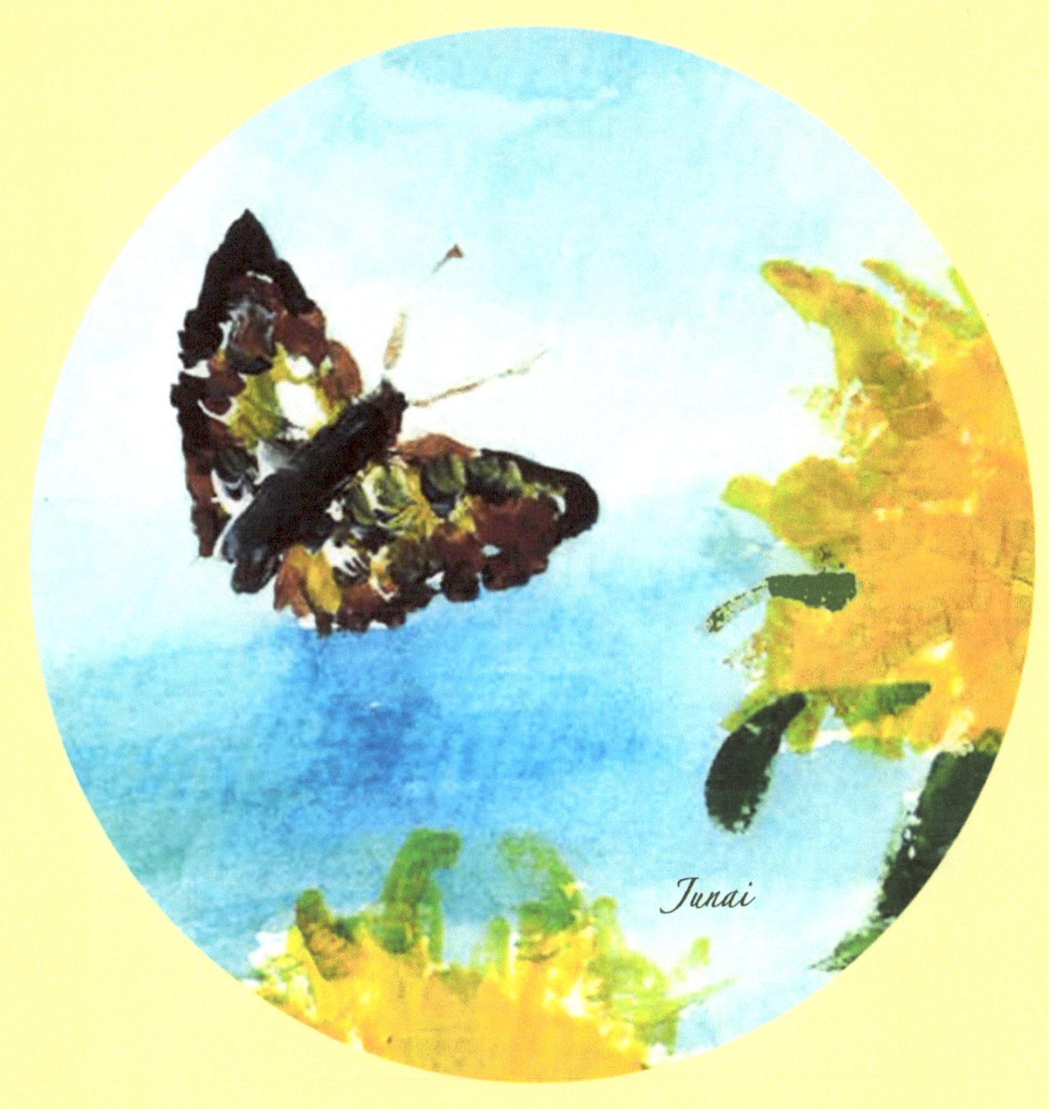

vital

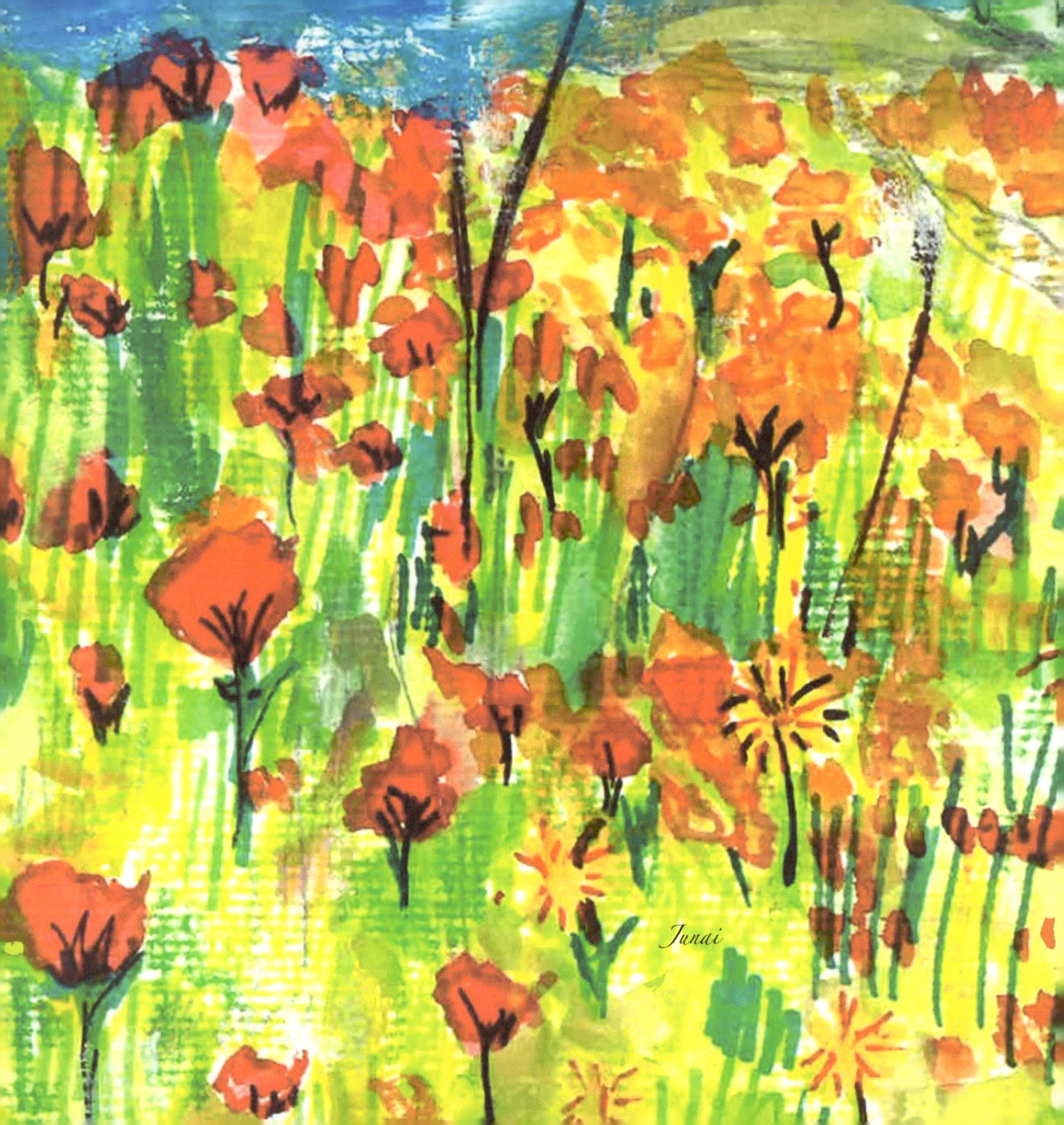
Junai

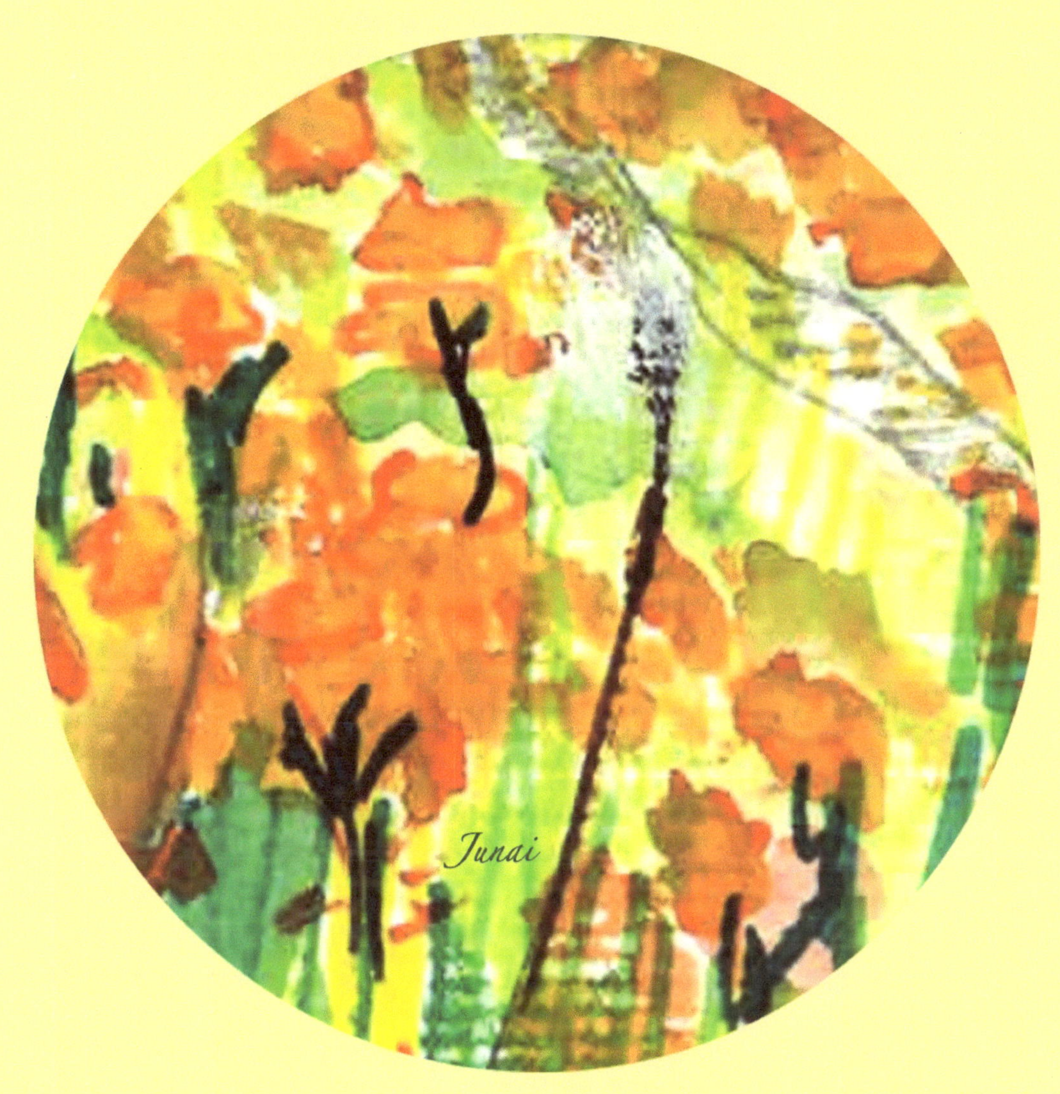

willing

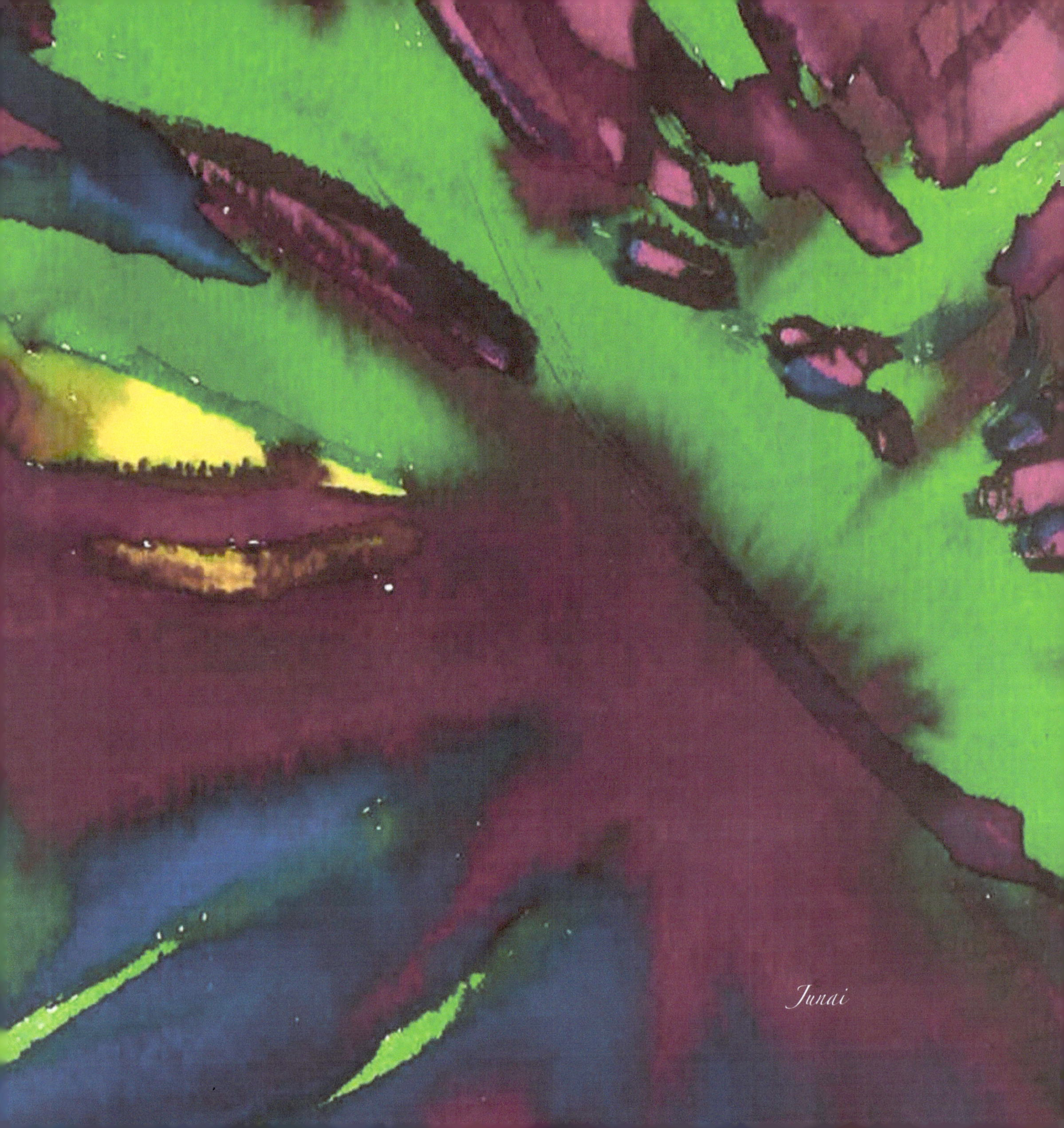
Junai

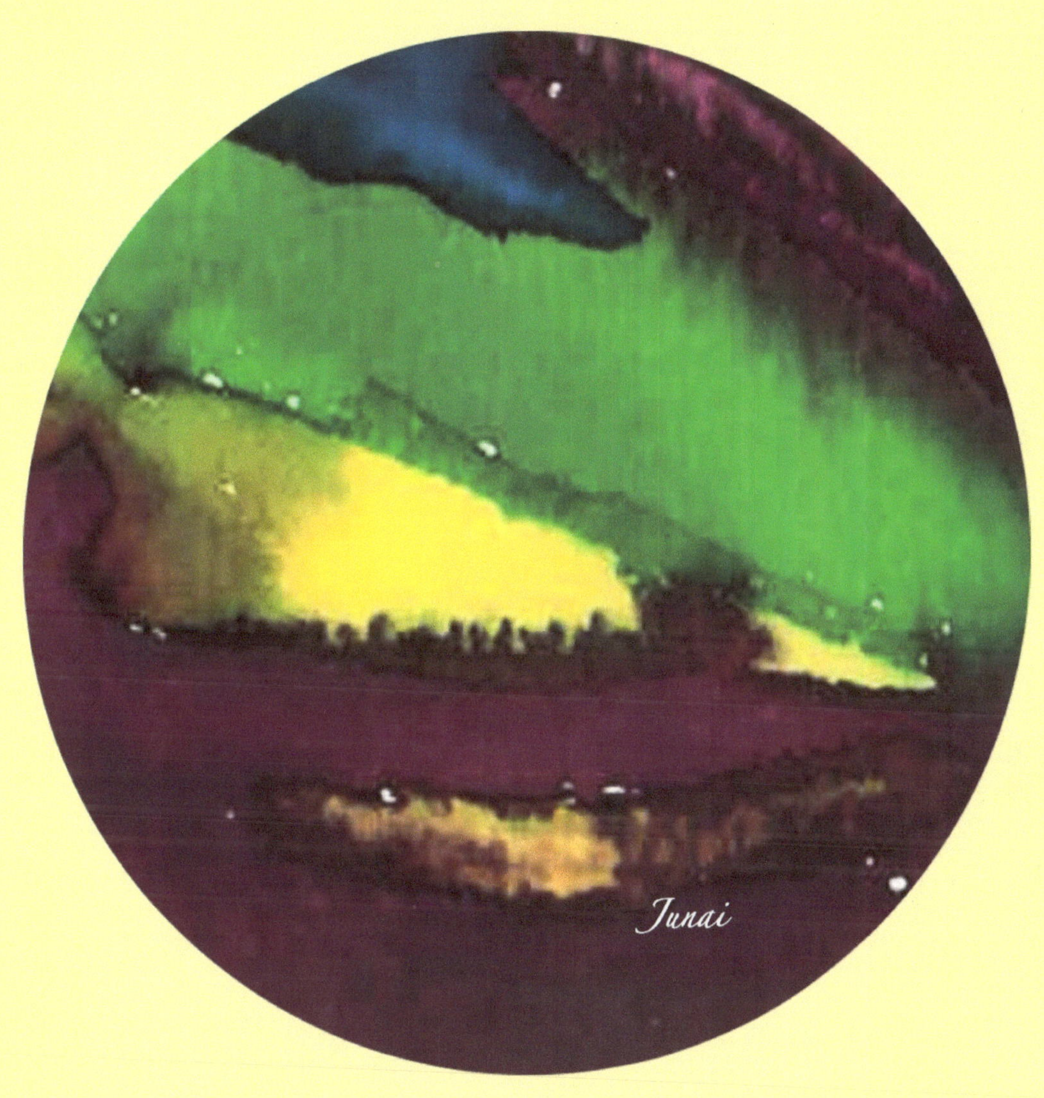

eXuberant

Junai

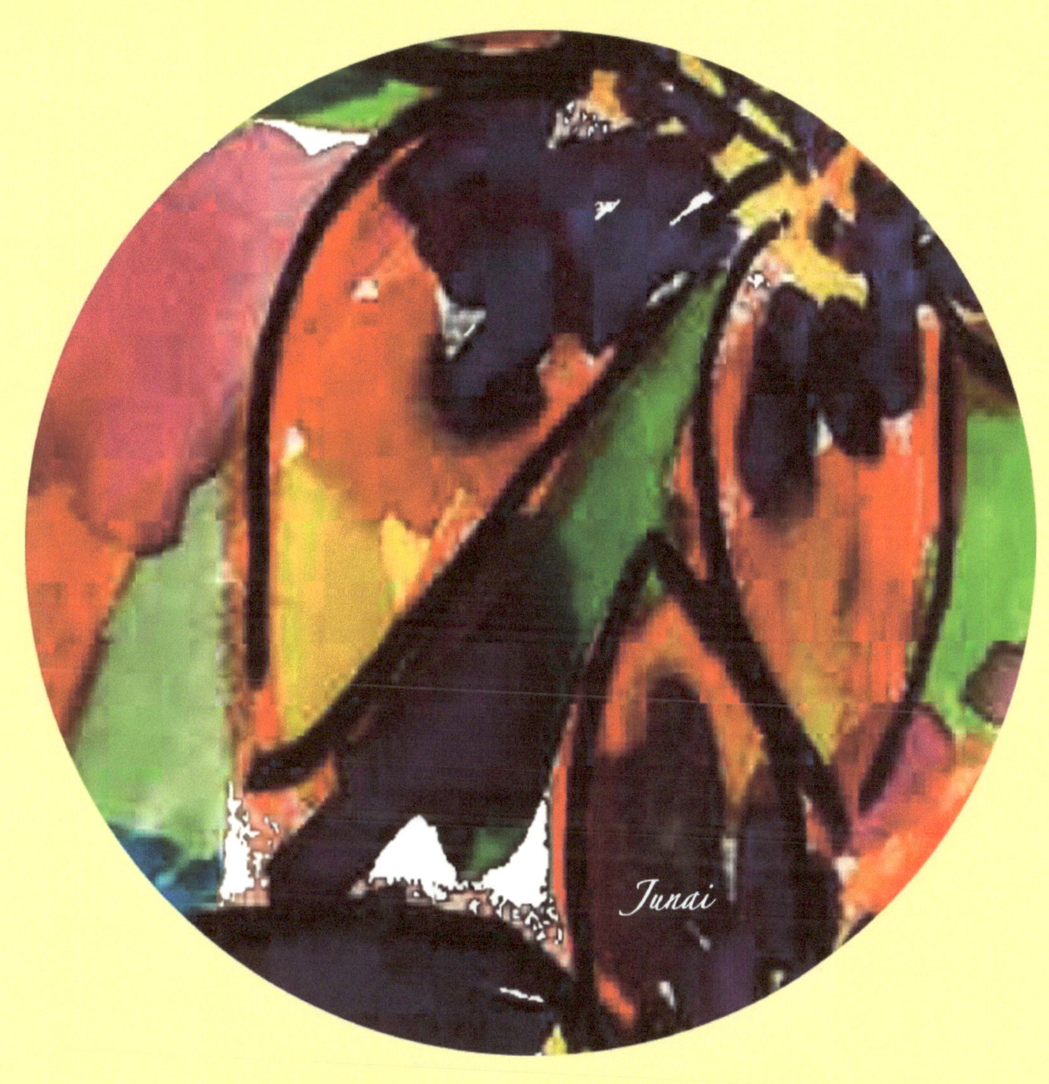

youthful

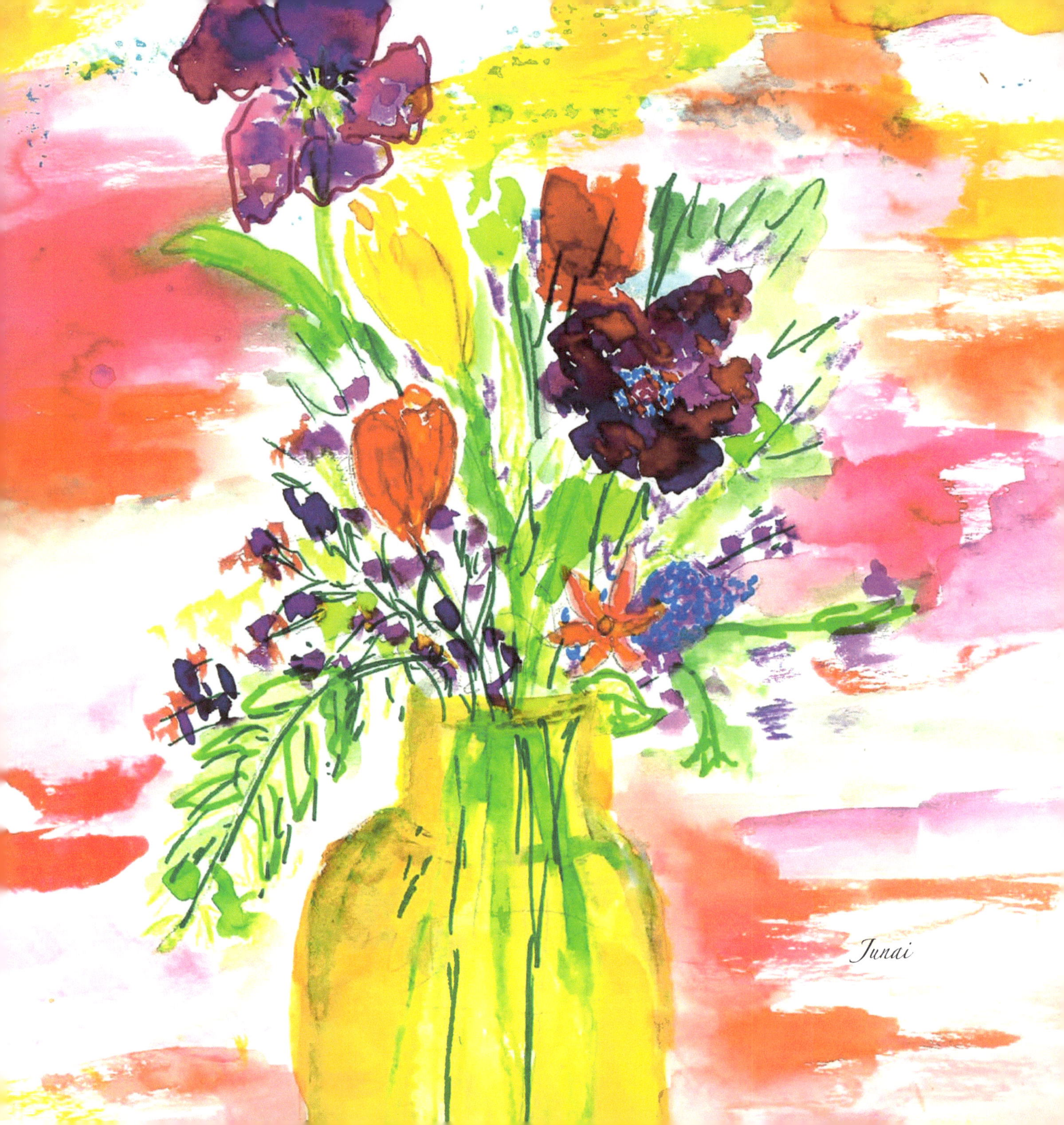
Junai

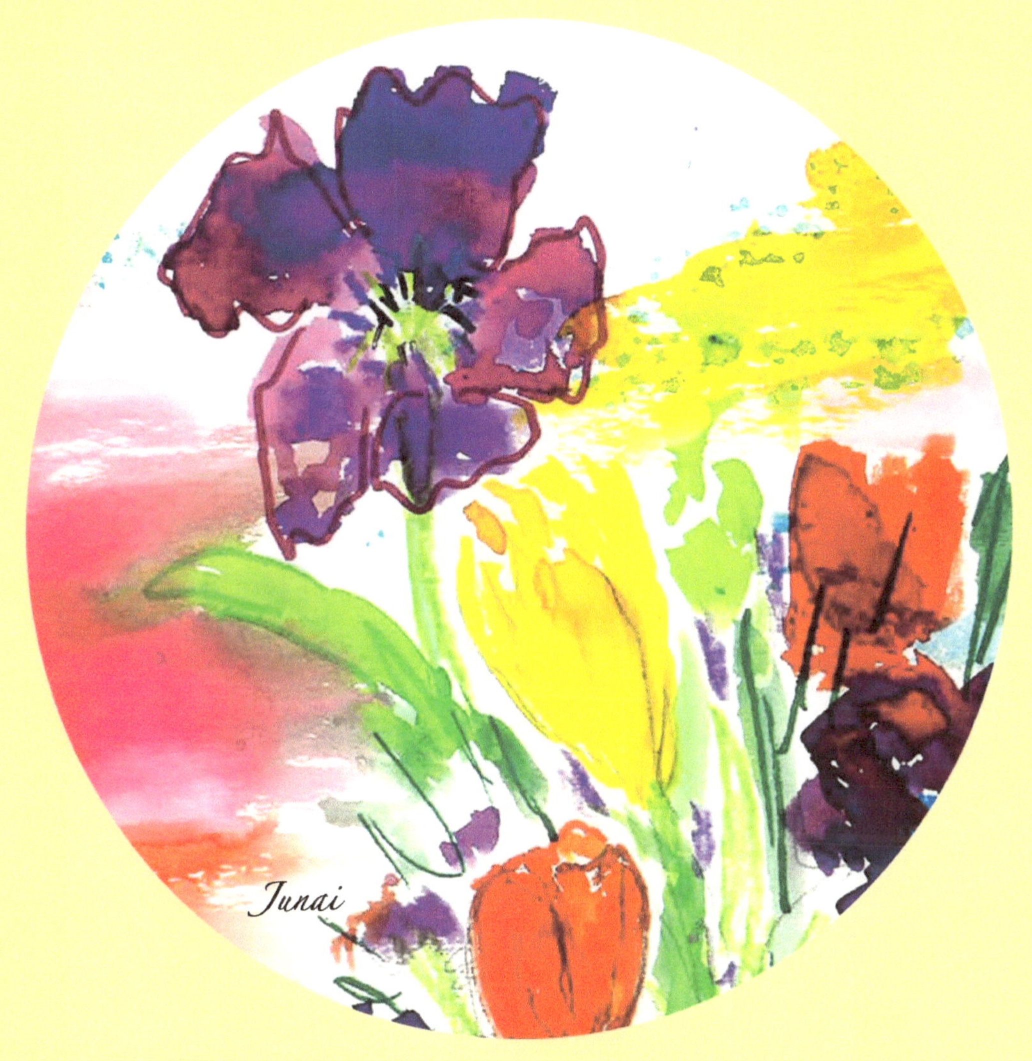

zealous

Love never ends.
Love never ends.
Love never ends.
Love never ends.

Follow the author, Mary Rensberry, at:
www.maryrensberry.wordpress.com

Her other books include:

It's Black and White/Navigating the ADHD Controversy
co-authored with her husband, Richard Rensberry

Fowl Art-prose with artist's pictures

Nature's Gift to Humanity-more prose with unique art

Christmas Christmas Everyday-Why wait until the holidays to give the gift of love to others? It can be experienced everyday of the year.

Be sure to check out some of the other books written or illustrated by Mary Rensberry and her husband, Richard, at QuickTurtle Books LLC® and found on Amazon:

1. **Monster Monster**-about a child's imagination at night

2. **If I Were a Garden**-a children's book of rhyme about being in the garden

3. **I am a Spirit/The ABC's of an Ideal Spirit**-a pictorial display of our inherent traits and virtues

4. **Christmas Christmas Everyday**-From the Everyday Series Collection® about sharing the Christmas spirit each day

5. **How the Snake Got Its Tail**-about living a clean life free of drugs

6. **Colors Talk**-about the colors of the rainbow and what they say

7. **If I Were a Lighthouse**-A Rhyme for Young Readers about what lighthouses do to help others

8. **I Wish It Were Christmas**-about a tree wanting to share its gifts to the world

9. **Goblin's Goop**-a modern day Battle of Jericho story about the environmental evils of pesticides and the company who makes them

10. **If I Were a Book**-about what joys a book brings to those that read

11. **If I Were a Heart**-a child's book of rhyme about a loving heart

12. **The Blind Dove**-(The Wings of God)-a book about having a disability but yet having other gifts that most people do not use

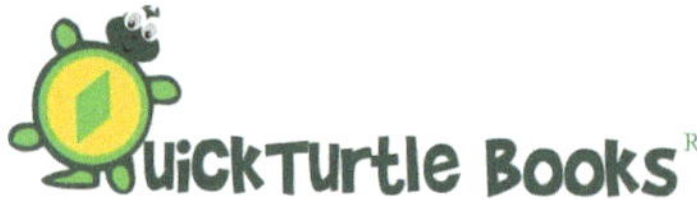

www.ingramcontent.com/pod-product-compliance
Lightning Source LLC
LaVergne TN
LVHW070147110826
845147LV00002B/340

* 9 7 8 1 9 4 0 7 3 6 2 5 9 *